Hear Me

When I

CALL

Hear Me When I CALL

When I

Connecting with a God Who Cares

CHARLES R. SWINDOLL

WORTHY
PUBLISHING

Published by Worthy Publishing, a division of Worthy Media, Inc., 134 Franklin Road, Suite 200, Brentwood, Tennessee 37027.

HELPING PEOPLE EXPERIENCE THE HEART OF GOD

eBook available wherever digital books are sold.

ISBN: 978-1-936034-93-2 (hardcover w/ jacket)
ISBN: 978-1-936034-85-7 (international edition)

Unless otherwise noted, Scripture quotations are taken from the New American Standard Bible®, © The Lockman Foundation 1960, 1962, 1963, 1968, 1971, 1972, 1973, 1975, 1977, 1995. Used by permission.

Other Scripture quotations are taken from the following sources: The Holy Bible, New International Version® (NIV), copyright © 1973, 1978, 1984, 2011 by Biblica, Inc.™ Used by permission of Zondervan. All rights reserved worldwide. www.zondervan.com. *The Message* by Eugene H. Peterson (MSG). © 1993, 1994, 1995, 1996, 2000. Used by permission of NavPress Publishing Group. All rights reserved. Good News Translation® (GNT), Today's English Version, second edition, © 1992 by American Bible Society. All rights reserved. J. B. Phillips: The New Testament in Modern English, Revised Edition. © J. B. Phillips 1958, 1960, 1972. Used by permission of Macmillan Publishing Co., Inc. The King James Version of the Bible (KJV). Public domain.

Quote from J. Oswald Sanders in the introduction is taken from J. Oswald Sanders, *Spiritual Leadership* (Chicago: Moody, 1980), 103.

A portion of this book was derived from the previously published *The Prayers of Charles R. Swindoll*, Volumes 1 and 2.

Published in association with Yates & Yates, www.yates2.com

For foreign and subsidiary rights, contact Riggins International Rights Services, Inc.; rigginsrights.com

Cover and Interior Design: Susan Browne Design
Cover Image: © Getty Images; AVTG and JayneBurfordPhotography

Printed in the United States of America

13 14 15 16 17 CGFF 8 7 6 5 4 3 2 1

It is with great gratitude I dedicate this book

to the congregation of Stonebriar Community Church

with whom I pray each time we gather

to worship our awesome God.

CONTENTS

INTRODUCTION

After more than five decades of ministry, I've come to the conclusion that prayer is the easiest and, at the same time, the most difficult discipline a follower of Christ can engage in. It's easy because it involves something we do every day: talking. That's what prayer is, talking with God. J. Oswald Sanders, in his wonderful book *Spiritual Leadership*, wrote, "Prayer is the most ancient, most universal, most intensive expression of the religious instinct. It touches infinite extremes, for it is at once the simplest form of speech that infant lips can try and the sublimest strains that reach the Majesty on high. It is indeed the Christian's vital breath and native air."

But prayer is also difficult. Why do we find it hard to "breathe"? Perhaps some of us are too lazy or impatient. Others of us are too embarrassed or ashamed to speak to God, thinking our petty problems too insignificant to bother the Lord of the universe. For many, and let's be honest here, prayer seems like we're only talking into thin air or whispering in an empty room. We know God is present and hears our prayers, yet we have a strange feeling of distance and isolation.

There's a near-truism among Christians that reveals much about our view and practice of prayer: "When all else fails, try God." We make a reliable habit of praying as a last resort when life turns to chaos. Otherwise, prayer remains a sporadic and occasional exercise. But why? We know that through prayer we have access to the source of power. We know that God intervenes. We know that God honors it when we pause from our work, turn our hearts heavenward, and say, "Lord, You take over." Why is it, then, that we pray only when we're seized with panic or when we come to the end of our own resources?

I confess that the longer I live, the more rebuked I am over my own prayerlessness. I would love to tell you that I am a model of continued, constant, faithful prayer. I am a man of prayer. I do believe in prayer. But I am no different from anyone else. Many times, prayer is what I try only when everything else has failed. So I understand. We all need help, myself included. Sometimes it's just hard to articulate what is within the depths of our hearts.

My hope is that this volume will help you put into words what your heart and soul are trying to say to the Lord. This collection of ninety prayers, selected from my years of ministry experience, is offered not because I consider myself eloquent but in hopes that they might minister to you in your need—as if we're praying them together. I encourage you to do more than just read these prayers—make them your own. To help you do that, I have included a devotional following each prayer to stimulate your thinking. I am extremely grateful to Wayne Stiles for his excellent assistance in helping me shape these devotionals into more meaningful and personal statements. It is our hope that these prayers and devotionals encourage you to make your entire life a prayer to God.

As you spend time in these pages, may you find the lungs of your prayer life beginning to fill with ever deepening and refreshing air. So breathe . . . breathe deeply, as you spend time in the fresh air surrounding those all-important, intimate moments with God.

—Chuck Swindoll

Frisco, Texas

1

New Year

SEEK FIRST HIS KINGDOM AND HIS RIGHTEOUSNESS, AND ALL
THESE THINGS WILL BE ADDED TO YOU. —MATTHEW 6:33

HOW FAITHFUL YOU HAVE BEEN, *our Father, over the many weeks of this past year. We pause to commit our lives to Your Son, Jesus Christ, afresh and anew, as if for the first time. We are thankful for the joy of knowing You and for those occasions during this past year when we have met You in unexpected ways. As we stand on the threshold of a new year, we thank You in advance for the fifty-two weeks that stretch out before us. Knowing that You are in charge, we accept whatever they may include.*

We will seek first Your kingdom and Your righteousness this year, knowing that all the other things we need will be added to these. Help us throughout the new year to stay focused on the eternal, rather than becoming distracted by and anxious over the temporal. As You meet our needs—not our greeds—teach us contentment, joy, happiness, and fulfillment in the realities of life that only You make possible. As opportunities and privileges unfold before us this year, we pray You would find us faithful. After all, our lives are Yours . . . and so it is right that we commit them to You.

We pray in the magnificent name of Jesus, who gave His life for ours. Amen.

See also Proverbs 27:1; 2 Corinthians 5:15; James 4:13–14.

———————— ‿ ————————

DON'T JUST SIT THERE

Sandwiched between January 1 and December 31 are twelve exciting months filled with possibilities. Challenges brought on by changes await us. We will be shoved out of our comfort zones and required to respond. We can do so positively or negatively, with hope and optimism or with resentment and pessimism. If we're not careful, we'll be so full of complaining that we'll miss golden opportunities to grow . . . to make some new discoveries . . . to switch from being a passive sitter to an active participant in our adventure beyond the familiar.

Between doing nothing and trying something ridiculous, there's a wide expanse worth considering. Whatever we choose to do, just sitting there isn't an option.

Seeing fifty-two weeks all wrapped and ready to be opened and knowing each one contains surprises that will require adjustments, I suggest we decide right now to open them with great anticipation. Let's also accept them with great delight. Think of the dozens of things God will teach us and the many ways we'll see Him work! Frankly, I have found that my "youth is renewed like the eagle" (Psalm 103:5) when I'm willing to change and make the necessary adjustments. Breaking out of an old, tired routine is one of the secrets of staying young.

Go there. Better still, let's go there together! By the end of this year, you and I will discover that God had several amazing things for us that we would never have known or experienced had we not accepted the challenge that changes inevitably bring.

It's time to take on whatever these new weeks and months will bring. The main thing for us to remember? Don't just sit there!

2

The Antidote to Apprehension

BE ANXIOUS FOR NOTHING, BUT IN EVERYTHING BY PRAYER
AND SUPPLICATION WITH THANKSGIVING LET YOUR REQUESTS
BE MADE KNOWN TO GOD. AND THE PEACE OF GOD, WHICH
SURPASSES ALL COMPREHENSION, WILL GUARD YOUR HEARTS
AND YOUR MINDS IN CHRIST JESUS. —PHILIPPIANS 4:6–7

———————— ❧ ————————

WE ALL EXPERIENCE APPREHENSION, *Father. How help-*
ful it is to remember we are to celebrate Your name, Your work, Your
power, Your character—all day, every day—so we might come to the
place where we revel in You. What a grand reminder it is that Your
Son could come at any moment. May You find us ready for that, Lord.

Yet we cannot be ready for Your return as long as anxiety lives
within us, so we pray that You will begin to do a work right now in
our lives to rid us of worry. What a waste that we have spent so much
of our lives fretting and worrying!

Remind us today and in the days to come that prayer can displace our apprehensions. Time with You can become such a magnificent turning point, not only in the moment but in the day—in fact, in our lives—so that we begin to realize the power of Your peace as it calms us. Give us the ability, the discipline of mind, to meditate on and focus our attention toward that which is true and noble, reputable and authentic, compelling and gracious. In the marvelous name of Christ, our Savior, we pray. Amen.

See also Psalm 37:5; 55:22; Jeremiah 17:8; Matthew 6:26–34.

APPREHENSION

A pprehension is everywhere. It's in the classroom when the new teacher makes her first attempt to connect with middle-school students. It's in the cramped study of the final-year med student as she crams the night before her orals. There's apprehension at the airport as a dad waves good-bye to his son leaving for overseas duty. Or in the nursery at night as an exhausted mother holds her sick baby. Or in the car traveling cross-country as a family relocates to an unfamiliar neighborhood.

Apprehension. It's a cut above worry but feels like its twin. It isn't strong enough to cause fear, but neither is it weak enough to be funny. It's a mixed emotion . . . and we've all felt it.

In some ways apprehension leaves us crippled, even paralyzed. It's an undefined uneasiness . . . a feeling of uncertainty . . . misgiving . . . unrest. What frustration is to yesterday, apprehension is to tomorrow.

Truth be told, apprehension is proof positive we're human. But unfortunately, it tends to smother our pleasant dreams by placing a pillow over our faith. Apprehension will strap a short leash on our vision and teach us to roll over and play dead when scary statistics whistle and pessimistic reports snap their fingers.

The apostle Paul refused to run when apprehension haunted him. He openly acknowledged its presence but stood his ground with the exhortation to the Philippians: "Be anxious for nothing" (4:6). Apprehension is intimidating until godly determination pulls rank and forces it to salute. Especially when determination has been commissioned by the King of kings.

3

Assurance of Salvation

MY SHEEP HEAR MY VOICE, AND I KNOW THEM, AND
THEY FOLLOW ME; AND I GIVE ETERNAL LIFE TO THEM,
AND THEY WILL NEVER PERISH; AND NO ONE WILL SNATCH
THEM OUT OF MY HAND. —JOHN 10:27–28

GRACIOUS FATHER, THE BEAUTY *of the natural world and
its elements that obey You remind us that we serve a living Savior.
These things tell us that You are very much alive and in full control.
The life around us reminds us that Your Son has been raised from the
dead. Nature testifies to Your work in the world as well as Your care
for Your creation. While this should soothe our doubts about You, Your
promises, and Your power, all too often it doesn't.*

*We desire to be renewed within. We are totally dependent upon
You to do that, to effect in us the renewal that we cannot accomplish
within ourselves. Enlighten the dark shadows and give truth where
now ignorance and superstition and fear abide. Replace our many*

doubts with assurance of our great salvation. Increase our faith. May it not be dependent upon the flimsy and fragile web of feelings but upon the solid granite of Your truth.

And having done that, give us a song that brightens our day and lightens our way. Help us to live in Your truth that removes our burden of doubt.

In the name of Christ, to whom we give first place, we pray. Amen.

See also Colossians 2:1–3; Hebrews 3:14; 6:11; 10:22; 11:1; 1 John 5:11–13.

A BENEDICTION OF ASSURANCE

I love the powerful promise recorded in Jude 24–25: "Now to Him who is able to keep you from stumbling, and to make you stand in the presence of His glory blameless with great joy, to the only God our Savior, through Jesus Christ our Lord, be glory, majesty, dominion and authority, before all time and now and forever. Amen."

This benediction builds upon the hope of our Savior's coming for us, as it tells us something our Lord is doing for us now . . . as well as something He will do for us then, when He comes.

Now: He is keeping us from stumbling (v. 24).

Then: He will present us "blameless with great joy" (v. 24).

Currently, He is guarding us, protecting us, securing us, and helping us not to stumble. How He loves us and reassures us! How often He strengthens us when we are weak!

When our dear Lord returns, we will be blameless . . . faultless . . . flawless. Jesus will not be angry because of our failures and ready to shame us. Instead, the grace we experience *now* we will also have *then* in abundance.

You would think the Almighty would frown as He reviews a large clipboard with your name above a list of the numerous times you stumbled. No—a thousand times, no! God keeps no such records against you. Rest assured.

He will accept you in that day, being fully aware that you are but dust . . . and He will escort you into the presence of His glory "blameless." I invite you to stop this moment and think that over. It's not possible to imagine the scene without smiling, seized with inexpressible joy.

4

Turning Bitterness into Sweetness

EVEN IF YOU SHOULD SUFFER FOR THE SAKE OF RIGHTEOUSNESS, YOU ARE BLESSED. AND DO NOT FEAR THEIR INTIMIDATION, AND DO NOT BE TROUBLED, BUT SANCTIFY CHRIST AS LORD IN YOUR HEARTS, ALWAYS BEING READY TO MAKE A DEFENSE TO EVERYONE WHO ASKS YOU TO GIVE AN ACCOUNT FOR THE HOPE THAT IS IN YOU, YET WITH GENTLENESS AND REVERENCE; AND KEEP A GOOD CONSCIENCE SO THAT IN THE THING IN WHICH YOU ARE SLANDERED, THOSE WHO REVILE YOUR GOOD BEHAVIOR IN CHRIST WILL BE PUT TO SHAME. —1 PETER 3:14–16

OUR FATHER, AS WE ACKNOWLEDGE *Your Son as Lord over all, it is with a sigh, because we cannot deny the pain or ignore the difficulty of our earthly trials. This reality can sometimes be borderline unbearable. But as the sovereign One with full capacity to handle our needs, You are strong enough to carry our burden and, in return, to give us the perspective we need.*

Quiet our spirits. Give us a sense of relief as we face the inevitable facts that life is difficult and there will be moments when life is not at all fair. Erase any hint of bitterness. Enable us to see beyond the present, to focus on the invisible, and to recognize that You are always with us. Remind us that Your ways are higher and far more profound than ours.

Thank You for the joy of this day. Thank You for the pleasure of a relationship with You and with a few good, caring, loving friends. And especially, Father, thank You for the truth of Your Word that lives and abides forever.

In the strong name of Him who is higher, Jesus our Lord, we pray. Amen.

See also Proverbs 14:19; 15:1; Ephesians 4:31–32; Hebrews 12:14–15; James 1:19–20.

BITTERNESS

The book of Hebrews states that a "root of bitterness" can spring up and cause trouble (12:15). We cannot nurture bitterness and at the same time conceal it. At times we think we can hide our bitterness, but we cannot. Worst of all, you, the victim of bitterness, will be the most miserable.

Consider Jesus' parable recorded in Matthew 18:23–35. The main character is a man who refused to forgive a friend . . . even though he, himself, had recently been released from an enormous debt. Because he refused to forgive his friend, the man was "handed . . . over to the torturers." (v. 34). Then Jesus added the punch line: "My heavenly Father will also do the same to you, if each of you does not forgive his brother from your heart" (v. 35).

Jesus said that we who refuse to forgive—we who live in bitterness—will become victims of torture, meaning inner torture and torment by all sorts of thoughts and feelings. Please remember: Jesus was speaking to His disciples, not to the unsaved. Christians suffer terribly until we fully forgive others . . . even when others are in the wrong.

We can now understand why Paul listed bitterness *first* when he said, "Let all bitterness and wrath and anger and clamor and slander be put away from you, along with all malice. Be kind to one another, tender-hearted, forgiving each other, just as God in Christ also has forgiven you" (Ephesians 4:31–32).

For your sake, I urge you to put away all bitterness. We must diligently pull up every root of bitterness. Let's do that now.

5

Anticipating His Return

FOR OUR CITIZENSHIP IS IN HEAVEN, FROM WHICH ALSO WE EAGERLY WAIT FOR A SAVIOR, THE LORD JESUS CHRIST. —PHILIPPIANS 3:20

FATHER, WE ARE DELIGHTED *with the sure expectation of Your Son's return. Thank You for telling us Your plan and not leaving us in a hopeless quandary. At the same time, thank You for not telling us everything. If every last detail of Jesus' return were spelled out, who would need to walk by faith? What would hold our attention and capture our curiosity, especially in those moments on this earth that suddenly remind us, this could be the day?*

Thank You also for giving us instruction that prepares us for eternity with You. Thank You, Father, for Your Son, who completed His mission while He was on this earth and will return for us at any moment.

We thank You for the joy that floods us when we anticipate such an event. The cares of this age finally will be gone. The crippling diseases, the painful trials, and the clammy fingers of death around our necks will be gone, gone forever! Heartbreaks, broken promises, and sorrows will all pass away when we are brought face-to-face with the Savior. How wonderful! We exult in this, Lord. And we praise Your wonderful name for including us in Your eternal plans.

Even so, come quickly, Lord Jesus. Amen.

See also Psalm 21:6; 98:1–9; Isaiah 26:19; 1 Thessalonians 2:19.

CHRIST'S RETURN MADE PRACTICAL

The other evening my wife and I were enjoying a quiet conversation together. For some reason our discussion turned to the subject of Christ's return. We kept returning to the thought, "He is coming back. What a difference it will make!"

It is amazing what a mental overhaul that does on our scale of values. Christ's return has a way of thumping us back to the basics, doesn't it? How much time do we spend on things that really do need attention . . . but would abruptly blur out of focus at the sound of the trumpet? God seemed to be saying to me that evening, *Loosen your grip, My son, and remember that the bottom line of everything is eternity with Me.*

When is the last time you—on your own—meditated on that fact? If you're like me, it's been too long. People who are more practical than mystical, who are more realistic than idealistic, tend to save thoughts of eternity for funerals or near-death experiences. Most of us are here-and-now thinkers more than there-and-then people.

Hear this: the *someday* return of Christ has tremendous implications on *today*.

Let's consider a few examples to get our thinking started. Live every day (as if it's your last) for His glory. Work diligently on your job and in your home (as if He isn't coming for another ten years) for His name's sake. Share the good news of Jesus every chance you get . . . and remain balanced, cheerful, winsome, and stable.

May we anticipate His return day after day after day.

6

Cleansing in the Depth of God's Word

BE GRACIOUS TO ME, O GOD, ACCORDING TO YOUR
LOVINGKINDNESS; ACCORDING TO THE GREATNESS OF YOUR
COMPASSION BLOT OUT MY TRANSGRESSIONS. WASH ME THOROUGHLY
FROM MY INIQUITY AND CLEANSE ME FROM MY SIN. —PSALM 51:1–2

OUR FATHER, IN A DRY AND BARREN WORLD *where sin
is rampant and society is filthy, we need a fountain of fresh, clean
water full of blessing, truth, and strength. We need water that's never
bitter . . . always sweet to the taste. Most of all, we need You. "Come
Thou fount of every blessing."*

*In a world that has no song to sing and whose stories are often
coarse and vulgar, we need a new song. Teach us to sing Your songs of
praise from our hearts, reengaging our minds to things that are pure
and holy and good and right and just and lovely and of good report.*

We are thirsty today for Your living water. May it cleanse us.

May it wash our minds. May it purify our motives. May it scrub away the shameful secrets of our private worlds so that You can lead us onto right paths. Admittedly, we are "prone to wander . . . prone to leave the God we love." And only the cleansing, fresh water of Your Spirit can make us clean deep within.

Make us clean today, our Father. Dig deeply into our lives and reveal truth. Find within us no rival, no resistance, no pride, no lies. We now give ourselves to Your sacred work, to be set apart for Your best use, for Your greater glory. In the name of Jesus, we pray. Amen.

See also Proverbs 20:9; Jeremiah 33:8; Ezekiel 36:25; 2 Corinthians 7:1.

THE DEPTHS

Anyone who loves the sea has a romance with it as well as a respect for it.

The romance of the sea is difficult to describe. It is nurtured in the shallow waters near the beach. The thundering waves have such a powerful magnetism that we cannot resist giving them our cares as the prevailing winds blow away all reminders of our responsibilities. And oceans that are miles deep with their massive swells are intriguing.

The romance of the shallows changes to respect at the depths. Who hasn't felt an uneasy churning in the midst of angry swells? When we can no longer see land and the depth gauge fails to register the fathoms, something profound reaches within us. On the surface of such waters we have little to say . . . yet our thoughts, like the measureless miles beneath us, become deep. We hold our breath, stare at the black brine, and let the wonder in. We treat the mystery of the deep with silent respect.

What is hidden in the sea is also hidden in God's wisdom. Perhaps Paul had recently been in the ocean when he wrote, "the Spirit searches all things, even the depths of God" (1 Corinthians 2:10).

The depths. Those fathomless truths *about* Him and those profound insights *from* Him produce within us a wisdom that enables us to think *with* Him. Such wisdom comes from His Spirit, who alone can plumb the depths and reveal His mind. God grants wisdom only to those who wait in silence . . . who respect "the depths of God." It takes time. It calls for solitude.

There is more than enough noise in the bottom of the boat, so let's not add to it. I suggest we climb on deck, get alone, and gain new respect for the depth of God's wisdom in His Word.

7

Living the Truth

As those who have been chosen of God, holy and beloved, put on a heart of compassion, kindness, humility, gentleness and patience; bearing with one another, and forgiving each other, whoever has a complaint against anyone; just as the Lord forgave you, so also should you. . . . Whatever you do in word or deed, do all in the name of the Lord Jesus, giving thanks through Him to God the Father. —Colossians 3:12–13, 17

You have written these words *to us today, Father. Though they date back to the first century, they fit the twenty-first century like a well-tailored garment. They touch every aspect of our being. Your words address our position in Christ and our practice on earth. They specify our struggles without overlooking the important, positive side of compassion, love, forgiveness, patience, humility, and gentleness. How we long to live as we say we believe. How far short of* *that we often fall! We realize it again even this day, as we recognize the straight line of truth so clearly marked in Your inspired Word—God-breathed, preserved, and now provided for us in our language. Help us to live according to Your standards, day in, day out.*

As You do soul-surgery in our hearts, may we allow the scalpel of the Spirit to pierce whatever area needs to be addressed. Guard us from hypocrisy. Few things are more detestable than a phony Christian! May we speak truth today. More importantly, may we live truth today. May we declare it to others in a way that makes sense. May Your Spirit take it from there and drive it home. May our lives and theirs be changed as a result.

In the name of Jesus Christ, we offer our words of prayer. Amen.

See also Psalm 1:1; 89:14; Hosea 14:9; Ephesians 4:15; Hebrews 13:8.

———————— ༚ ————————

CONSISTENCY

onsistency. We can count on it. It will be there tomorrow just like it was yesterday . . . free from mood swings, unexpected changes, or fickle fads. Early in the day or late at night, consistency stands firm. When pain or hardship bites, consistency doesn't bleed. When the majority is tired and irritable, consistency is stable and resilient. Not insensitive or boring, but reliable and faithful. Not opposed to reason, but trustworthy. Not stubborn, but solid. Yes, that's it: *solid*.

Consistency is the stuff most mothers are made of when their little ones get sick . . . and missionaries who lose themselves in their labor even though it yields limited fruit. It reveals itself in faithful employees who show up on time, roll up their sleeves, and commit to doing the job rather than watching the clock. Diligence is its brother . . . dependability, its partner . . . discipline, its parent.

Consistency. A living model of patience, determination, and strength—regardless of shifty, rootless times. The blasts of ridicule and criticism may punch it in the face—but consistency stands and takes it as silently as a bronze statue takes the tempest. It's an obvious mark of maturity. It's hanging in there day in and day out in spite of everything that could get us sidetracked.

One of the most attractive, magnetic characteristics of Christ is His consistency. When you need Him, He is there. He's there even when you don't think you need Him! You're never too early or too late. He's never in a lousy mood, nor will He ask you to call back during office hours. He's available because He's immutable. With Him there's no yesterday or tomorrow, no new year or old year. He is "the same," regardless (Hebrews 13:8). Isn't that wonderful?

<u>8</u>

Controlling Our Words

SEE HOW GREAT A FOREST IS SET AFLAME BY SUCH A SMALL FIRE!
AND THE TONGUE IS A FIRE, THE VERY WORLD OF INIQUITY;
THE TONGUE IS SET AMONG OUR MEMBERS AS THAT WHICH
DEFILES THE ENTIRE BODY, AND SETS ON FIRE THE COURSE
OF OUR LIFE, AND IS SET ON FIRE BY HELL. —JAMES 3:5–6

———————— ✍ ————————

OUR FATHER, OUR TONGUES *are far too often wicked and
out of control! We have breached confidences that were meant to be
held in trust. We have told several people of the offense we received
but have failed to speak with the offender to make things right. And
we have spoken jealous and envious words of one who was promoted
over us. Many lack the courage to tell us to our face of our error,
but You don't; You command us to get control of our tongues. We're
rebuked by Your indictment: from the same mouth come both blessing
and cursing . . . these things ought not to be this way.*

Lord, help us to remember that there's no decision more impor-

tant than salvation. And on the heels of that, there's no decision more important than the decision to restore a relationship that has been fractured because of hurtful words. Forgive us for speaking before we knew the facts or before we earned the right to say what we've said. Forgive us for hurting a brother or a sister who wasn't even there to defend himself or herself. Hear our prayer today and vindicate us, Lord, for we, too, have been verbally assassinated and our integrity has been violated. And we ask You to fight our battle for us.

We come to You today in faith in the name of Jesus Christ our Lord. And with our tongues we say amen.

See also Psalm 120:1–4; Proverbs 16:27–28; Luke 6:37–38; James 3:8–12.

THE LAW OF ECHOES

Echoes are one of the immutable laws of physical nature—and especially of human nature. What do I mean? We get in return *exactly* what we give. It all comes back, sometimes in greater measure than we gave. Remember what Jesus once said? "By your standard of measure it will be measured to you in return" (Luke 6:38).

The law of echoes applies to a *marriage*. You want a wife who is gracious, forgiving, tolerant, and supportive? Start with her husband!

Apply the words of our Savior and treat her exactly as you would like her to treat you (Matthew 7:12). Exactly. That's quite a promise, but it rests on quite an assignment.

The law of echoes applies to our *work* as well. The rocky canyons within the lives of others are ready to echo back the identical attitudes and actions we initiate. Want your associates at work to be cheery and unselfish, free from caustic comments and ugly glares? The place to begin is with that person you see in the bathroom mirror each morning.

It's remarkable how consistent this law remains. Pupils in a classroom are usually echoes of the teacher. A congregation of worshippers is usually a reflection of the preacher. If the one communicating is negative, sour, blunt, and demanding . . . the echo reflects those same characteristics, almost without exception.

The law of echoes. If we want others to judge and condemn us, we start it. If we want them to be understanding, broad-minded, allowing us room to be ourselves—then we begin by being that way. Like begets like. Smiles breed smiles. Laughter is contagious. Unfortunately, so are frowns and harsh, abrasive words. Whatever we deposit we draw out in return. Sometimes *more!*

9

Courage for the Discouraged

I WAITED PATIENTLY FOR THE LORD; AND HE INCLINED TO ME AND HEARD MY CRY. HE BROUGHT ME UP OUT OF THE PIT OF DESTRUCTION, OUT OF THE MIRY CLAY, AND HE SET MY FEET UPON A ROCK MAKING MY FOOTSTEPS FIRM. —PSALM 40:1–2

LORD, BRING US RELIEF *when we are swamped with the ever-rising tide of discouragement. Grant deliverance for us who are caught in that swamp and start to slide into its slimy waters. Encourage our hearts as we face those depressing, dark moments that leave us feeling hopeless and believing the lie that things will never change. Father, give us hope beyond our heartbreaks. We cling to the inspired words of the apostle Peter that if we humble ourselves before the mighty hand of God, You will lift us up. You will exalt us at the proper time. Discouragement keeps us humble, we confess, for we are never discouraged and bigheaded at the same time.*

Father, lift our spirits by transforming our minds. Strengthen us to see the value of dwelling on things that are true, honest, just, pure, lovely, and of good report. Help us to fix our minds on heavenly things rather than on earthly things that drag us down.

Thank You that Christ loves us and keeps on loving us. Thank You that while we were yet sinners, Christ died for us. Thank You that the grace that saved us keeps us saved . . . regardless of our doubts.

We also pray for those weary souls who have never met Your Son as Savior. We ask that their burden of discouragement be lifted by the realization that Jesus' death on the cross paid the complete price for their sins. Help them see past their pain to the reality that there is nothing they need to do or promise or change or give up or become in order to be accepted by You. Just simply trust in Your Son. May they do that today. In Your name we pray. Amen.

See also Psalm 69:1–4; Daniel 4:36–37; Acts 16:31; Romans 5:8; 12:2;
Philippians 4:8; Colossians 3:1–4; 1 Peter 5:6.

THE CURE FOR DISAPPOINTMENTS

There is a fly in the ointment of disappointments. We put it there. So there's nobody to blame but ourselves. Stop and think it over. What causes us to be disappointed? We had it all set up in our mind and anticipated a certain outcome or response, but it never materialized.

We need to take an honest look at the one thing that inevitably leads to disappointments: our *expectations*. We erect mental images that are unrealistic or unfair or biased. Those images become our inner focus, rigidly and traditionally maintained. Leaving no room for flexibility on the part of the other person (allowing no place for circumstantial change or surprise), we set in mental concrete the way things must go. When they *don't*, we either tumble or grumble . . . or both.

The result is tragic. The radius of our toleration is greatly reduced. Our willingness to accept others' imperfections or a less-than-ideal circumstance is blocked. And—worst of all—the delightful spontaneity of a friendship gets strained. The chain of obligation, built with the links of expectations, binds us in the dungeon of disappointment.

We need to give one another stretching room. Room to respond in a variety of ways. This will require burning our list of expectations. It will also mean we stop anticipating the *ideal* and start living with the *real*, which is always checkered with failure, imperfection, and even *wrong*. So instead of biting and devouring one another, let's serve one another in love (Galatians 5:13, 15). I don't know of a better way to kill the flies that spread the disease of disappointment.

10

Daily Doubts

[JESUS] SAID TO THOMAS, "REACH HERE WITH YOUR
FINGER, AND SEE MY HANDS; AND REACH HERE YOUR HAND
AND PUT IT INTO MY SIDE; AND DO NOT BE UNBELIEVING,
BUT BELIEVING." THOMAS ANSWERED AND SAID TO HIM,
"MY LORD AND MY GOD!" —JOHN 20:27–28

———————— ༄ ————————

OUR FATHER, ENCOURAGE US—*especially we who often doubt and feel ashamed of that. May we realize that You are in the midst of our reflections and through such inner searching we can come to new insights and depths that we would otherwise never have known.*

Thank You for preserving the story of Thomas. We see ourselves portrayed so vividly in his doubts. May we realize that You're pleased even in our searching and You honor our honest questions. Thank You for accepting us in our struggles and understanding our doubts. Thank You for Your grace in understanding that though we weep when we lose our friends and family, and we question the tragedies and calamities of life, it isn't that we doubt Your right to rule. It's that we struggle with releasing our own rights. We're simply trying to reason our way through that mysterious valley.

Father, we wish to know You as we've never known You before. May today be the beginning of increasing trust and decreasing doubts.

We ask this in the rock-solid name of Jesus, our Lord and our God. Amen.

See also Matthew 14:28–33; James 1:5–8; Jude 22.

FAREWELL, DOUBT AND DISILLUSIONMENT

The prophet was in the pits. Literally. Swamped with disillusionment and drowning in despair, he cursed the day he was born (Jeremiah 20:18). An exaggeration? Hardly. Jeremiah's journal holds nothing back. The chief officer in the temple had God's prophet whipped with forty lashes and then placed in stocks. Why? Had he committed some crime? No. He had simply declared the truth—and this is what he got in return.

The man is in anguish. Prophet or not, he is struggling with God's justice. Deep down he is questioning God's presence. "Where is He? Why has the Lord vanished at a time when I need Him the most?"

The ancient man of God is not alone with feelings like that. Who hasn't wrestled with similar questions and doubts? Sometimes they come in the long, dark tunnel of suffering when the pain won't go away. Or when a marriage partner who promised to stay "for better or for worse" breaks that vow. Or when a long-sought-after dream goes up in smoke. Or when we kiss a loved one good-bye for the last time.

At those times I'm tempted, like Jeremiah, to hang it up. But right about the time I start to jump, I experience what Jeremiah admitted: "Then in my heart it becomes like a burning fire shut up in my bones; and I am weary of holding it in, and I cannot endure it" (Jeremiah 20:9).

Directly sent from God is this strong surge of hope, confidence, and determination swelling up within me. The disillusionment is quietly replaced with His reassurance. Clarity has returned. Divine perspective has provided a fresh breeze of hope in the pits. In those moments, I have determined that disillusionment must go. Now . . . not later.

11

Hope beyond Failure

JUST AS HE WAS SPEAKING, THE ROOSTER CROWED. THE
LORD TURNED AND LOOKED STRAIGHT AT PETER. THEN
PETER REMEMBERED THE WORD THE LORD HAD SPOKEN
TO HIM: "BEFORE THE ROOSTER CROWS TODAY, YOU
WILL DISOWN ME THREE TIMES." AND [PETER] WENT
OUTSIDE AND WEPT BITTERLY. —LUKE 22:60–62 NIV

———————— ✦ ————————

DEAR FATHER, EVERY ONE OF US *has experienced failure.*
Many *failures. Our failures have left us broken, depressed, disappointed in ourselves, and full of regret. Flashbacks of those episodes
haunt us. How distressed we can feel in those moments! Thank You
for the transformation made possible by forgiveness. Thank You for
understanding that we are but dust, often incapable of keeping our
own promises or living up to our own expectations.*

*Renew our hope as we reflect on Peter, with whom we so easily
identify. Remind us that just as You used Peter after his failures, You*

will also use us by Your grace. May our memories of failure bring about a humility that sees Your grace as what it really is . . . amazing.

Help us find fresh encouragement and new strength from Your Word. We look to You alone for the ability to hope again. Only You have the power to make something beautiful and good out of lives that are littered with the debris of thoughts we should never have entertained . . . words we should never have said . . . and deeds we should never have done.

Our only source of relief comes through Your grace. Bring it to our attention again and again in those critical moments when discouragement does a number on us . . . and make us grateful. In the gracious name of Jesus, we ask this. Amen.

See also Psalm 32:1–11; Micah 7:19; John 21:15–19; Romans 8:28.

SUCCESSFUL FAILURES

I'll never forget that day, many years ago. Evel Knievel launched in his "sky cycle" to jump the Snake River Canyon. He barely made it off the launch pad before his parachute opened . . . and landed him gently in the river. The stunt was a first-class flop. Yet he walked away from his failure with a smile, a bulging wallet, and his pride still intact. Nobody in the long history of sports ever came off a more abysmal failure better than Evel Knievel.

I see an abiding truth: *the person who succeeds is not the one who holds back, fearing failure, nor the one who never fails . . . but rather the one who moves on in spite of failure.*

Give me a sky cycle with all its risks any day rather than sentence me to the path of predictability between the rock walls of routine and fear. God asks that we believe Him *regardless* of the risks, in spite of the dangers, ignoring the odds. Nineveh experienced a revival because Jonah—a recent spiritual dropout who smelled like fish—brought them the message. The Gentiles heard of Jesus because Paul got up after being knocked down. And Peter's two letters are in the Bible because he refused to live in the shadow of his failure . . . in spite of the roosters he heard each morning.

Those who aim for—and successfully attain—great achievements are usually those who missed many times before. Our failures, you see, are only temporary tests along the way to prepare us for magnificent triumphs.

Wherever you are today, trust me: sitting there licking your wounds will only result in a bitter taste in your mouth. Sighs and tears and thoughts of quitting are understandable for the moment but inexcusable for the future. Let's get up and get on with it!

12

Remembering That God Is Faithful

REMEMBER MY AFFLICTION AND MY WANDERING, THE WORMWOOD AND BITTERNESS. SURELY MY SOUL REMEMBERS AND IS BOWED DOWN WITHIN ME. THIS I RECALL TO MY MIND, THEREFORE I HAVE HOPE. THE LORD'S LOVINGKINDNESSES INDEED NEVER CEASE, FOR HIS COMPASSIONS NEVER FAIL. THEY ARE NEW EVERY MORNING; GREAT IS YOUR FAITHFULNESS. —LAMENTATIONS 3:19–23

LORD GOD, THANK YOU *for being more than a friend. Thank You for Your sovereign hand upon us, for Your mercies that are new every morning, for Your great faithfulness. Thank You for not leaving us when we should have been rejected and left, for not abandoning us when we deserved it. Thank You for being true to Your Word. Thank You for keeping Your promise that all who come to You will in no way be cast out. Thank You, our Shepherd, for Your sheepdogs—that is, for goodness and mercy and, especially, faithfulness—*

that follow unrelenting at our heels. In faithfulness, You will receive those who come to You.

We pray for those who have run away from You. We urge You to win them back through Your compassion and mercy. We ask that they would sense the sympathetic faithfulness of God and that alone would draw them like a magnet to You.

In the name of Christ, our strong Savior, we pray. Amen.

See also Numbers 23:19; Psalm 23:6; 139:5, 16; Isaiah 45:9; 46:9–10; Daniel 4:35; Zephaniah 3:5; John 6:37; Hebrews 10:23.

———————— ت ————————

MERCY BRINGS RELIEF

The essential link between God's grace and our peace is mercy— God's infinite compassion actively demonstrated toward the miserable. Not just pity. Not simply sorrow or an understanding of our plight . . . but divine relief that results in peace deep within.

Paul, after admitting that he was "formerly a blasphemer and a persecutor and a violent aggressor," was allowed to become a participant in the service of the King. How? He explains in four words: "I was shown mercy" (1 Timothy 1:13).

The ancient Hebrews had a word they used most often for mercy—*chesed*, pronounced "kesed." It refers to God's loyal love and is frequently translated "kindness" and "lovingkindness." There are many "miseries" to which mercy brings needed relief.

When we're suffering the pain of unjust consequences (Genesis 39:21–23).

When we're enduring the grief of a death (Ruth 1:8–9).

When we're struggling with the limitations of a disability (2 Samuel 9).

When we are hurting physically (Job 10:12).

When we're under a cloud of guilt after we've sinned (Psalm 32:10; 51:1).

Remember the familiar words of Psalm 23? Unless we read that psalm through the eyes of a sheep, we'll miss its magnificent message. It concludes, "Surely goodness and mercy shall follow me all the days of my life" (KJV). Think of goodness and mercy as God's sheepdogs. They stay with us, right on our heels, "all the days of our lives." What helpful companions! There is no unfair consequence too extreme for mercy. No grief too deep. No handicap too debilitating. No pain too excruciating. No sin too shameful. Sheep are often in need. That's why mercy, our faithful companion, stays near.

13

The Family

LIKE ARROWS IN THE HAND OF A WARRIOR, SO ARE THE CHILDREN

OF ONE'S YOUTH. HOW BLESSED IS THE MAN WHOSE QUIVER

IS FULL OF THEM; THEY WILL NOT BE ASHAMED WHEN THEY

SPEAK WITH THEIR ENEMIES IN THE GATE. —PSALM 127:4–5

MARRIAGE. A HUSBAND AND WIFE *coming together as one. Family. Rearing children. These things are so much of what life is about, our Father. They give us hours of pleasure . . . and hours of frustration. There's probably nothing that most of us work harder at and sometimes feel guiltier about than our family. What a mystery! Yet You have it all figured out. Somewhere between what You wrote and what we do, there's been a breakdown. We need help. We know it won't be easy or quick, but it'll come as we learn from You. Help us unlearn our many habits and patterns that are not in line with Your Word and will. Forgive us for having clung to them.*

We like things that make sense. We like things that have a clear ring to them. We like things that help us feel good. But often, Lord, the things You have to say about marriage and family are none of the above. That's tough for us to handle, especially when we feel like we're swimming against the stream. We work with people who scoff at marriage. We live around people who are unfaithful in their marriages. We struggle in our own concepts of marriage. Help us, Lord.

With confidence, we commit our families to You. In Jesus' name. Amen.

See also Exodus 20:12; Deuteronomy 6:6–7; Proverbs 1:8; Colossians 3:18–20.

———————— ◡◠ ————————

IT'S TIME TO TAKE TIME

Years ago my older son, then a teenager, and I dropped by the local Hallmark gift shop to find a card for Mother's Day. As I roamed across the endless field of choices, Curt got bored and wandered back to the posters.

After a while he called for me to come look at one he had found. It was a large picture of a boat in the middle of a very still lake, either at dawn or dusk. A father was sitting at one end, the son at the other, both fishing. Tiny circlets of ripples surrounded each cork as the lines stretched lazily from pole to water. Both were smiling and obviously enjoying those leisure hours together. Two words were neatly printed at the bottom of that exquisite scene of solitude: *TAKE TIME*.

The memory of that moment causes me to pause . . . occasionally at birthdays . . . often at anniversaries . . . and especially at holidays. Do you ever stop on these days and think about the importance of taking time for your family? Please do.

If we're not careful, we will spend those special days preoccupied in a squirrel cage of activities and distractions. Please don't. With long hours of free time sitting there unaccountable, we'll be tempted to fill them with "necessary" work projects, a half-dozen piddling little time-consuming assignments, preoccupied for hours with our smartphone, or even a whole day hanging out with a few of our buddies. Not good choices.

Stop before saying yes to any of the above. Instead, let's ask ourselves, "Why not spend some quiet time with one of my kids?" or maybe, "Shouldn't my family get my undivided attention for a change?" It's time for us to take time.

14

A Prayer for Fathers

A FATHER OF THE FATHERLESS AND A JUDGE FOR THE WIDOWS, IS GOD IN HIS HOLY HABITATION. GOD MAKES A HOME FOR THE LONELY; HE LEADS OUT THE PRISONERS INTO PROSPERITY, ONLY THE REBELLIOUS DWELL IN A PARCHED LAND. —PSALM 68:5–6

LORD, YOU ARE GOOD *to give us fathers. Far too often it's a difficult role and thankless job. Therefore, we pray that You would encourage all the men in that position today. Guard their hearts. Strengthen their resolve. Help them embrace the joy that comes with rearing their children.*

We thank You for our own fathers. For those of us who had supportive, loving, and faithful fathers, we give You thanks. There is nothing like a good father—one who leads his family with love and grace, presenting a life of self-sacrificial love consistently to his children.

Father, we also pray today for those who haven't a father nearby or didn't have a father like they would have wanted. We pray You would make them trusting people, to see that You are the Father of the fatherless. You're able to take their deepest hurts and heal them. We pray You would use Your Word and Your people to help relieve some of that pain. For those who have not yet bowed their knee to the Savior, bring them to that place right now.

May this be a day in which we give honor to You, God, for giving us our fathers. In the name of Christ, we pray. Amen.

See also Exodus 20:12; Proverbs 4:1; 13:1; Luke 11:11–13.

FATHERS

For the next several minutes, think about your father. Meditate on what that one man contributed to your life. Think about his influence over you, his investment in you, his insights to you. Study his face . . . the image now indelibly etched in your mind. Listen again to the echo of his voice . . . that infectious laugh . . . those unique expressions that emerge through the miracle of memory. Feel his hand wrapped around yours . . . his strong, secure arm across your shoulders. Remember his grip that once communicated a balanced mixture of gentleness and determination . . . compassion and masculinity.

Best of all, take time to recall his character—especially if he was a man of *integrity*. As you read this, pause and remind yourself of just one or two choice moments in your past when he stood alone as he stood by you . . . when he stood against insurmountable odds . . . when he provided that shelter in your time of storm. When he chose to say, "I forgive you," instead of, "You ought to be ashamed!"

In the wake of such a legacy which time can never erase, give God thanks. Thank the Giver of every good and perfect gift for the meaningful marks your dad has branded on the core of your character.

He is far from perfect. Painful though that fact is, he would be the first to admit it. Nor is he infallible, much to his own disappointment. Nor altogether fair . . . nor always right. But there's one thing he is—always and altogether—he is *your dad* . . . the only one you'll ever have.

Take it from me, the one thing he most needs to hear you say is, "Dad, I love you." If he is still living or accessible, call him and tell him. If he's no longer here, tell the Lord.

15

Overcoming Fear

Even though I walk through the valley of the shadow of death, I fear no evil, for You are with me; Your rod and Your staff, they comfort me. —Psalm 23:4

———————— ⟿ ————————

Lord God, fear threatens *to overtake us, to hinder us from trusting You. We often seek to rely on ourselves, trusting in our own strength to accomplish our own desires. Because we recognize the realities and the dangers of this distressed world, we thank You for making clear Your plan to ultimately remove all fear and anxiety and worry. Thank You for communicating the truth about fear in terms we can grasp. Thank You for challenging us to trust You as You unfold Your plan in the teaching of Scripture. Give us a commitment to Your truth so that we live differently and think differently. Help us to be passionate about what matters so that we care more about the eternal and less about the temporal.*

Shake us awake, our Father, with the reality that the world is heading in the wrong direction. Remind us that we have the oppor-

tunity to make a difference in the lives of people, despite the lawless

times . . . if we would but trust You. Deliver us from fear that holds

us back, that we might magnify the name of Jesus Christ, regardless

of our work, our calling, and our involvements. For Jesus' sake, we

pray. Amen.

See also Genesis 26:24; Deuteronomy 3:22; Psalm 46:1–2; Luke 12:7.

———————— ༺·༒ ————————

FACING FEAR WITH TRUTH

What a monster is fear! Its claws are sharp, dripping with the blood of the unknown and unseen. Its voice is piercing, shouting ugly and destructive words of worry. Most of its statements begin with a quiet, "What if . . ." and end with a loud, "You'll be sorry!" One blast of its awful breath transforms saints into practical atheists as fear reverses our entire mind-set. Its bite carries paralyzing venom into its victim, and it isn't long before doubt dulls our vision. As we fall, it steps on our face with the weight of a military boot . . . and laughs at our crippled condition as it prepares for another assault.

Fear. Ever met this beast? Sure you have. It comes in all shapes and every size. Fear of failure. Fear of crowds. Fear of disease and death. Fear of rejection. Fear of unemployment. Fear of what others are saying about you. Fear of moving away. Fear of height or depth or distance. Fear of trusting others. Fear of being yourself. Fear of buying. Fear of selling. Fear of financial reversal. Fear of the dark. Fear of war. Fear of business failure. Around every imaginable corner fear lurks in the shadows, planning to poison your inner peace and outward poise.

David's Twenty-third Psalm scratches the fearful where they itch. With broad, bold strokes of his pen, the shepherd boy puts iron in our bones. He meets fear at the door with one simple statement: "Even though I walk through the valley of the shadow of death, I fear no evil, for You are with me" (Psalm 23:4).

Oh, how I need to claim this truth in moments of fear! Maybe you do too.

16

Endurance in Trials

BE STRONG AND COURAGEOUS, DO NOT BE AFRAID OR TREMBLE AT
THEM, FOR THE LORD YOUR GOD IS THE ONE WHO GOES WITH YOU.
HE WILL NOT FAIL YOU OR FORSAKE YOU. —DEUTERONOMY 31:6

———————— ༄ ————————

LORD, WE ALL REMEMBER TIMES *of passing through the
waters and going through the fire—overwhelming tests and furnace-
like trials. And we have the scars to prove it. As those times return,
we trust You that the waters will not drown us and the fire will not
burn us. How faithful You are, Lord, to meet us at every one of life's
contingencies . . . how caring and accepting, how full of grace and
mercy. It is because of Your mercies that we are not consumed.*

*Now, Lord, do a work deep within our hearts. Provide us with
fortitude for the trials of life—those we're enduring and those on the
horizon. Help us come to terms with negative attitudes that have
been anchors weighing us down and stealing our joy. Forgive us for
the sour responses we have expressed and have encouraged in others.*

Give us eyes of faith to see beyond the predictable, beyond the facts and figures. Open us to a whole world of possibilities because You are the God of the impossible. Encourage us, Father, with thoughts that send us into our future with hope and joy. And may our attitudes become encouraging and contagious rather than destructive and poisonous.

In the name of the Lord Jesus, we ask these things. Amen.

See also 2 Samuel 10:12; Psalm 27:14; Isaiah 43:1–3; Matthew 14:27; Galatians 6:9; 1 Corinthians 15:58; 1 Peter 5:8, 10.

FINISHING WELL

Not enough is said or written today about finishing well. A tremendous amount of material is available on motivation to get started and creative ways to spark initiative. Plenty of advice is floating around on setting goals and establishing priorities and developing a game plan. All of it is insightful and needed.

But let's hear it for the opposite end for a change. Let's extol the virtues of sticking with something until it is done. Of hanging tough when the excitement and fun fade into discipline and guts. Not losing heart even though the project has lost its appeal.

I fear our generation has come dangerously near an I'm-getting-tired-so-I'll-just-quit mentality. Dieting is a discipline, so we stay fat.

Finishing school is a hassle, so we bail out. Cultivating a close relationship is painful, so we back off. Writing a book is demanding, so we stop short. Sticking with an occupation is tough, so we look elsewhere. Marriage is demanding, so we walk away.

Do I write today to a few weary pilgrims? Is the road getting long and hope wearing a little thin? Determine to finish well. Many start the Christian life like a lightning flash—hot, fast, and dazzling. But how many people age seventy-five and over can you name who are finishing the course with sustained enthusiasm? Oh, there are some, I realize, but why so few? What happens along the way that swells the ranks of quitters?

I really wish I knew that answer. If I did, I'd shout warnings from the pulpit Sunday after Sunday. No, better than that, I'd stoop over and whisper them to every discouraged person I meet. Before it is too late.

17

Willingness to Express Generosity

MANY WILL SEEK THE FAVOR OF A GENEROUS MAN, AND EVERY MAN IS A FRIEND TO HIM WHO GIVES GIFTS. —PROVERBS 19:6

———————— ∿ ————————

WE STAND BEFORE YOU, *our Father, as an act of allegiance and submission. And we bow before You in humility and trust. We desire to follow You. Every day, it's an uphill climb. It is often an internal battle to stand firm in what we believe and to model what You have asked of Your people in a world that is self-serving. Move in our hearts, so that our actions reveal change. May we practice acts of generosity over and above what we have ever considered.*

We pray that You will convince and convict us deep within, and that You will then find us as obedient in overflowing generosity. We are Your people. We are the sheep of Your pasture who belong to You—nothing is too difficult for You. So we pray that we will be able to focus our attention, our thoughts, and ultimately our will on what You have said, what You have promised, and how You will provide. May we be stimulated to good works in ways we have never known before.

And now, Father, we acknowledge that we have been the recipients of numerous benefits: blessing, healing, forgiveness, grace, mercy, even relief from guilt and shame and longstanding grudges we've held against others. We stand before You in allegiance and in submission, in generosity and joy. In the name of Jesus, our strong Savior, we pray. Amen.

See also Deuteronomy 15:10; Proverbs 11:25; Acts 20:35; 2 Corinthians 9:7;
1 Timothy 6:18; Hebrews 10:24.

GIVING WITH GUSTO

One statement Paul makes in the book of 2 Corinthians is perhaps the foundational Scripture reference linking joy with giving: "Each one must do just as he has purposed in his heart, not grudgingly [reluctantly] or under compulsion [feeling forced because of what others may say or think], for God loves a cheerful giver" (2 Corinthians 9:7). The term "cheerful" comes from the Greek term *hilaros*, from which we get our word *hilarious*. And it's placed first in the original statement for emphasis. Literally, "for the *hilarious* giver God prizes." Why? Because hilarious givers give with gusto!

Want to bring back the gusto? Let me remind you of two simple suggestions. Both work for me. First, *reflect on God's gifts to you.* Hasn't He been good? Always more than we deserve. Second, *trust God to honor consistent generosity.* Here's the big step, but it's essential. Go for it! Release your restraint—when you really believe God is leading you to make a significant contribution—and develop the habit of generosity. I seriously doubt that generosity has ever hurt anyone!

After Araunah offered King David something for nothing, the king replied, "I will not offer burnt offerings to the LORD my God which cost me nothing" (2 Samuel 24:24). David refused a handout. I love the application the great preacher of yesteryear, John Henry Jowett, drew from David's words, "Ministry that costs nothing, accomplishes nothing."

Let's give as we have never ever given before. Let's attack our indebtedness with great gusto. And let's also support God's work with outstanding offerings of a sacrificial nature. Remember: ministry that costs nothing, accomplishes nothing.

18

Generating a Gentle Spirit

IF WE LIVE BY THE SPIRIT, LET US ALSO WALK BY THE SPIRIT. LET US NOT BECOME BOASTFUL, CHALLENGING ONE ANOTHER, ENVYING ONE ANOTHER. BRETHREN, EVEN IF ANYONE IS CAUGHT IN ANY TRESPASS, YOU WHO ARE SPIRITUAL, RESTORE SUCH A ONE IN A SPIRIT OF GENTLENESS; EACH ONE LOOKING TO YOURSELF, SO THAT YOU TOO WILL NOT BE TEMPTED. BEAR ONE ANOTHER'S BURDENS, AND THEREBY FULFILL THE LAW OF CHRIST. —GALATIANS 5:25–6:2

———————— ꞊ ————————

WE ARE VERY THANKFUL, FATHER, *that in the process of our spiritual growth You remind us of the importance of gentleness. Your Word not only instructs us in what we're to do, but it also shows us how to do it. We remember what Paul wrote to the Thessalonians—that he gently dealt with them as a mother with a nursing child. Help us, Father, to have that kind of gracious, gentle spirit, especially those of us who tend to be impatient with others who are not as quick . . . or those of us who are healthy and lack compassion for others who are not as strong . . . or those of us who delight in accom-*

plishments but lack empathy for others who are not as productive.

It's so easy for all of us—if not verbally, at least in our minds—

to compete, to look down on others, to complain and to compare. May

we, through Your Spirit's power, become more like our gentle Savior,

whose yoke is easy and whose burden is light. Like our Master and

Lord, may our encounters with others be easy and bring light. Meet

our needs in a very special way, especially our need for a gentle and

quiet spirit.

In the name of Your gracious Son, we pray. Amen.

See also Matthew 5:5; 11:29–30; Galatians 5:22–23; 1 Thessalonians 2:7.

GENTLENESS

Gentleness seems an idea alien to the masculine temperament. The man portrayed in today's media is often rugged and hairy, is built like a linebacker, drives a slick sports car, and walks with a swagger. In the beer ads he's out for all the gusto in life. With women he is a conqueror. In business he's bullish. Even with a razor or hairdryer he's cocky. If you don't believe it, ask him! To the major-ity of young men—that's their hero, plain and simple.

Now let's understand something. A man *ought* to be a man! Few things turn us off quicker than a man who carries himself like a woman or wears clothes that suggest femininity. We are living in an era when gender roles are definitely eroding.

The right kind of toughness—strength of character—ought to mark the man of today . . . but not only that. *Gentleness* is equally important. So important, in fact, God places it on the list of qualities He feels should characterize every Christian: "But the fruit of the Spirit is love, joy, peace, patience, kindness, goodness, faithfulness, gentleness, self-control" (Galatians 5:22–23).

Gentleness has three close companions in the New Testament: love, meekness, and humility (1 Corinthians 4:21; 2 Corinthians 10:1; Ephesians 4:2). Furthermore, gentleness is the proper attitude when faced with three difficult assignments: exercising church discipline, facing personal opposition, and staying open to God's Word (Galatians 6:1; 2 Timothy 2:25; James 1:21).

Remember, our goal is always balance. Not either-or but both-and. Not just tough. That, alone, makes us cold, distant, intolerant, unbearable. Balance makes us tough and tender . . . gutsy and gentle, compassionate, thoughtful, teachable, considerate. Just like Jesus.

19

Godliness in a Godless Culture

DON'T YOU REALIZE THAT THIS IS NOT THE WAY TO LIVE? UNJUST PEOPLE WHO DON'T CARE ABOUT GOD WILL NOT BE JOINING IN HIS KINGDOM. THOSE WHO USE AND ABUSE EACH OTHER, USE AND ABUSE SEX, USE AND ABUSE THE EARTH AND EVERYTHING IN IT, DON'T QUALIFY AS CITIZENS IN GOD'S KINGDOM. A NUMBER OF YOU KNOW FROM EXPERIENCE WHAT I'M TALKING ABOUT, FOR NOT SO LONG AGO YOU WERE ON THAT LIST. SINCE THEN, YOU'VE BEEN CLEANED UP AND GIVEN A FRESH START BY JESUS, OUR MASTER, OUR MESSIAH, AND BY OUR GOD PRESENT IN US, THE SPIRIT. —1 CORINTHIANS 6:9–11 MSG

LORD GOD, YOUR SON *has closed yesterday's door, therefore Your people don't have to live enslaved to sin or shame anymore. Not because we've been strong and good and noble but because You have transformed our lives. You've changed our course of direction. Even though You've left us on foreign soil, as aliens and strangers, we have a home in heaven. And sometimes we get pretty homesick!*

Hear the prayers of Your people as we call out to You. Give us self-control on those occasions when we're tempted to moralize and put people down. Make us aware that a godly life preaches an unforgettable message to the unsaved. Help us remember that we are soldiers, away from our home in heaven, living in a culture that's lost its way and is in desperate need of Jesus Christ. Keep us easy to live with, strong in faith, unbending in our convictions yet full of grace toward those who are bound by sin and captured by habits they cannot break. Enable us to shock unbelievers with lives that are authentic, stay balanced, still have fun, and ultimately glorify You, God . . . just like Jesus did. In His great name, we pray. Amen.

See also John 15:18–19; 17:15–20; Romans 12:1–2; 1 Peter 2:11.

EVANGELICAL CARICATURES

To the world, Bible-toting evangelical Christians represent a host of confusing and contradictory concepts. We refer to being "born again," even though we reject reincarnation. We talk out loud to a Person we cannot see. We base our lives on a Book we believe

He wrote, though we didn't see Him do it. Our actions are even more inconsistent. Our worry list is long, though we claim He takes our burdens . . . our patience with the waitress is short, though she saw us pray . . . our driving is often thoughtless and lawless, though that bumper sticker identifies us as Christians. Color us red. Rather than that, give us masks. Better still, *make us invisible!*

You and I recognize those contrasts as the spiritual battle with the flesh. We leave room for such contradictions. But trust me, the unbeliever doesn't. He or she sees us through a distorted filter, formed from a jumble of exaggeration, confusion, and fact. Caricatures, admittedly, are false freaks, extreme representations. But they cause formidable hang-ups when the subject of Christianity is brought up.

The answer is not to try to be perfect (waste of time) or to peel off the "Jesus Is Lord" sticker (cop-out) so that all caricatures might be erased. Face it, some folks wouldn't change their erroneous ideas about Christians even if we lived like the apostle Paul. Even he had his critics.

Then what's the point? Only this. You can't change the model of other Christians. And you can't change the mind of other non-Christians. But you can do something about the lack of character inside *your* skin. The presence of caricatures doesn't matter nearly as much as the absence of character.

20

Gratitude for Grace

FOR THE GRACE OF GOD HAS APPEARED, BRINGING SALVATION
TO ALL MEN, INSTRUCTING US TO DENY UNGODLINESS AND
WORLDLY DESIRES AND TO LIVE SENSIBLY, RIGHTEOUSLY
AND GODLY IN THE PRESENT AGE. —TITUS 2:11–12

THANK YOU, DEAR LORD, *for the beautiful way You teach us. Thank You for Your patience when we fail. Thank You for Your understanding in the midst of all our own confusion. Thank You for reaching down to us when we would never have reached up to You. Thank You for stopping us when we were running in the wrong direction, for setting the Hound of heaven after us. Thank You especially for Your grace. For by grace we have been saved through faith; and that not of ourselves, it is the gift of God; not as a result of works, so that no one may boast. What a great reminder!*

Thank You, dear God, for being tough with us when we needed it, for disciplining us so that we would walk worthy of our calling.

How grateful we are that You have promised us a heavenly home free

of guilt and shame and sin and sorrow and death.

We look forward to eternity with You, with our Savior whom

having not seen, we love; in whom, though now we see Him not, yet

believing, we rejoice with joy unspeakable and full of glory. In the

great name of Jesus, we thank You. Amen.

See also Psalm 84:10–11; John 1:16; Ephesians 2:8–9; 1 Peter 1:8.

RECIPIENTS OF GRACE—ALL

Some folks go to great lengths to hide their humble origins. We often think we should mask the truth of our past, lest people think less of us—especially if our today is much more respectable than our yesterday. But the truth is, when we peel off our masks, others are usually not repelled; they are drawn closer to us. And frequently, the more painful or embarrassing our past, the greater is others' appreciation and respect.

The prophet Isaiah reminds us, "Look to the rock from which you were hewn and to the quarry from which you were dug" (Isaiah 51:1). That phrasing sounds much more noble and respectable than its literal meaning. The word "quarry," in the Hebrew text, actually refers to a "hole." The old King James Version doesn't miss it far: "the hole of the pit from whence ye are digged." Never forget "the hole of the pit." Excellent advice! Even those who are extolled and admired have "holes" from which they were dug:

- With Moses it was murder.
- With Elijah it was deep depression.
- With Peter it was public denial.
- With Samson it was recurring lust.
- With Thomas it was cynical doubting.
- With Jacob it was deception.
- With Rahab it was prostitution.
- With Jephthah it was his illegitimate birth.

Before we get enamored with our high-and-mighty importance, it's a good idea to take a backward glance at the "hole of the pit" from which Christ lifted us. And let's not just *think* about it; let's admit it. It has a way of keeping us all on the same level—recipients of grace.

21

Becoming Better Parents and Grandparents

FATHERS, DO NOT PROVOKE YOUR CHILDREN TO
ANGER, BUT BRING THEM UP IN THE DISCIPLINE AND
INSTRUCTION OF THE LORD. —EPHESIANS 6:4

THANK YOU, FATHER, FOR BEING *the perfect Parent.*
Thank You for those times You've taken us to task, though the reproof
sometimes seemed more than we could bear. Encourage us with the
truth that whomever You love You reprove, even as a father corrects
the son in whom he delights. Forgive us, our Father, for our prodigal
ways, for our selfish desires and self-willed decisions. Forgive us for
our pride in wanting to look like winners as parents when the truth
is we have failed at every point.

Help us to be real with our children—authentic, loving, forgiv-
ing, firm when we have to be, strong when we need to be, gentle at
all times. Help us, Lord. Help us with our grandchildren, to be there

for them when they need us, to be supportive and affirming of their parents, to be a part of the answer rather than a part of the problem. Enable us to come to terms with things that weren't dealt with in our own lives so that we don't pass them on to these precious children who follow us.

Lord, we give You thanks for the genius of the family. It's all Your idea. Give us very sensitive hearts as we grow in these areas of nurturing and discovery. In the dear name of Christ, we pray. Amen.

See also Deuteronomy 6:6–7; Proverbs 3:12; 22:6; Colossians 3:21; Hebrews 12:9–11.

GRANDPARENTING: A DEFINITION

Webster is kinda weird and hard to explain. Why? He omits *grandparenting* from his dictionary. That's somewhere between incompetent and inexcusable! Okay, okay, *grandparent* is there . . . so maybe *grandparenting* isn't an official word. Let's make it one.

Perhaps the best definition is a description. Grandparents' favorite gesture is open arms, and their favorite question is, "What do you wanna do?" They don't look for mistakes and failures; they overlook them. They don't remember that you spent your last dollar foolishly;

they forget it. And they don't skip pages when they read to you . . . nor do they say "Hurry up" when you want to see how far you can make the rock skip across the lake. They'll even stop and lick their ice cream cone as you lick yours.

Isn't God good? Generation after generation He provides a fresh set of grandparents . . . an ever-present counterculture in our busy world. Lest everyone else get so involved they no longer stop to smell the flowers or pat a dog or watch tiny ants hard at work, these unique adults are deposited into our lifestyle account. They've made enough errors to understand that perfectionism is a harsh taskmaster and that self-imposed guilt is a hardened killer. They could be superb instructors, but their best lessons are caught, not taught. Their Christianity is seasoned, filtered through the tight weave of realism, heartache, loss, compromise, and love. Jesus is not only their Lord; He's their Friend and longtime Counselor. Like a massive tree, they provide needed shade; they add beauty to the landscape; they don't mind being used. They're there. Even if not much is happening, they are there.

Even though Webster won't acknowledge the word, grandparenting is ours to enjoy . . . thoroughly and continually.

22

Growing toward Maturity

APPLYING ALL DILIGENCE, IN YOUR FAITH SUPPLY MORAL
EXCELLENCE, AND IN YOUR MORAL EXCELLENCE, KNOWLEDGE,
AND IN YOUR KNOWLEDGE, SELF-CONTROL, AND IN YOUR SELF-
CONTROL, PERSEVERANCE, AND IN YOUR PERSEVERANCE,
GODLINESS, AND IN YOUR GODLINESS, BROTHERLY KINDNESS,
AND IN YOUR BROTHERLY KINDNESS, LOVE. —2 PETER 1:5–7

———————— ও৴ ————————

FATHER, THANK YOU *for the character qualities that are such a vital part of our Christian lives. Though we bear very few of the marks of maturity Peter wrote about in the passage above, we always need to be stirred up by way of reminder. How often we have come before You, asking for help in these areas! You have heard our pleas on many occasions. Truth be told, You will hear them again. We yearn to be like Your Son, Jesus, the One who modeled each of these marks of maturity to perfection, though fully man. We long to grow in spiri-*

tual maturity . . . but the uphill journey takes so long. We confess that it often feels unending.

Thank You for the promise that Your Holy Spirit will be with us each step of the way. We desperately need His empowerment to keep us going and growing . . . until we become like Jesus . . . fully conformed to His image.

We ask, Father, that You give us hope beyond our immaturity. Help us in our unbelief. Guard us from discouragement. As we look back over the checklist You gave to Peter—and realize how far we have to go—remind us also how far we've come, by Your grace. Remind us that You will complete the good work You began in us . . . until the day of Christ Jesus. Through His matchless name, we pray. Amen.

See also John 14:16–17; Galatians 5:16; Philippians 1:6;
Hebrews 5:8; 1 Peter 1:10; 2 Peter 1:13.

GROWING UP

Growing old is not much of a challenge. All you have to do is keep on breathing. You don't have to think or exercise or read or take courses or travel or even get out of your own house. Just exist. It will happen automatically. Trust me; we will grow old with zero effort.

Growing *up*, however, is an uphill climb. We have to give it all we've got. To begin with, we can't let our attitude have its way. If we do, we'll get negative and crotchety. Also, our sense of humor will be squeezed out of us between the vise jaws of bad news and opinionated views. We'll find all kinds of people our age who have opted for a granite face that reflects suspicion, discouragement, monotony, resentment, and fear of risk. Furthermore, if we are really committed to growing *up*, we'll be forced to come to terms with a very painful fact: we can learn a lot from those who are younger . . . even little kids!

I read an article about a teacher who asked her class of ten-year-olds to write their observations of grown-ups. Each kid provided some awfully honest and interesting responses. Most of what I read amounted to this observation: *grown-ups don't do what they tell children to do.*

There is much to be learned from clear-thinking, honest-to-the-core children who see us as we are, no matter how hard we try to fake it. We're better people for listening.

Are we spending time around the young? Are we still listening and learning? If so, we deserve the title they reserve for adults only— but in our case, it really does mean *grown-up.*

23

Gratitude for God's Guidance

O LORD, LEAD ME IN YOUR RIGHTEOUSNESS BECAUSE OF MY FOES; MAKE YOUR WAY STRAIGHT BEFORE ME. —PSALM 5:8

OUR FATHER, FOR CENTURIES, You have used Your Word in the hearts of men and women in cultures and countries around this world. You have sent to difficult and obscure places faith-filled missionaries with the Word of God tucked away in their hearts. They have declared it, and You have blessed it. Your Word has spread like wildfire, and, as Your children, we are all recipients of Your faithfulness. Many of us had godly mothers and fathers who taught us the way from birth. Some of us learned the truth from mentors when we became adults. Others getting up in years discovered what they had been missing all their lives. We have been redeemed, bought by

Christ's blood, delivered from a life of bondage and addiction, and relieved of despair and slavery to sin. How grateful we are!

Thank You, Father, for leading us in our own personal exodus—leading us from start to finish, leading us when we didn't even want to know You, leading us even when we were running from You. Thank You for deliverance from the pharaohs of our lives—cruel taskmasters, all of them—and bringing us to the gentle Shepherd of our souls.

And so, Father, we pause at this moment in quiet worship to remember Your leading. We praise You in the name of Christ, our Savior and Lord. Amen.

See also Exodus 13:21; Psalm 25:5; 139:9–10; Isaiah 11:6.

LETTING THE LORD LEAD

There is a strange statement Paul made while he was saying good-bye to a group of friends. Most of the men were wiping away tears, realizing they would never see Paul again. Looking around, the aging apostle pointed south toward the Mediterranean Sea and voiced these words: "And now, in obedience to the Holy Spirit I am going to Jerusalem, not knowing what will happen to me there" (Acts 20:22 GNT).

What an honest admission! *"I am going . . . not knowing what will happen."*

In a compact nutshell, that's the Christian life, isn't it? Going . . . yet not knowing. As followers of our Lord we believe He leads us in a certain direction or in pursuit of a precise goal. That leading is unmistakably clear. At least, *to us*. So—out of sheer obedience— we go. We pack our bags, we pull up stakes, we bid friends farewell, and we strike out, facing a future that is as uncertain as the leading is sure. How strange . . . yet how typical!

There isn't a Christian reading my words who hasn't walked that path and struggled with ways to convince others it is right. And endured the frowns and well-meaning counsel of those who try to point out why the idea is a fluke, even downright dumb.

Who among our ranks hasn't stepped out on faith, leaving a sure thing, looking down a long, dark tunnel with no end in sight? And yet filled with unimaginable excitement! Going . . . yet not knowing. Obeying . . . yet not understanding. Beginning a journey based on faith that is unpredictable, risky, untried, and appearing virtually insane—yet prompted by none other than the Lord Himself. *That* is following Christ.

<u>24</u>

Striking a Chord of Harmony

THEREFORE I, THE PRISONER OF THE LORD, IMPLORE YOU TO
WALK IN A MANNER WORTHY OF THE CALLING WITH WHICH
YOU HAVE BEEN CALLED, WITH ALL HUMILITY AND GENTLENESS,
WITH PATIENCE, SHOWING TOLERANCE FOR ONE ANOTHER
IN LOVE, BEING DILIGENT TO PRESERVE THE UNITY OF THE
SPIRIT IN THE BOND OF PEACE. —EPHESIANS 4:1–3

LORD, WE REALIZE *that this is straight talk from You: "preserve
the unity of the Spirit in the bond of peace." It doesn't win votes,
but it gets attention. It doesn't promise that we'll get our way, but
it teaches truth. Your way is the best way . . . forbid that we ever go
any other way. We've tried those ways. We've discovered firsthand
that they're all dead-end streets or, if not that, they lead into dangerous swamps.*

So we pray that You will give Your people a sense of recommitment to this matter of unity and harmony and confidentiality and purity and love and tolerance and patience—in Your words, humility and gentleness in the bond of peace. May we model that, Lord. May we model that when we're at home, when we're in our neighborhoods, when we're at our workplaces, when we're behind the steering wheel of our cars, when we're doing business, when we're at the grocery store, when we're meeting new friends, and any other time we're given the opportunity to impact another life.

Give us great harmony, Lord. As You grow us up, grow us deep. May our roots deepen as our fruit ripens. In the name of Your dear Son, we pray. Amen.

See also Proverbs 10:11–12; John 13:34–35; 1 John 2:9–11; 4:7–9.

DIVERSITY AND UNITY

God has not made Christians all the same. He never intended to. Each of us has our own set of capabilities in which we will naturally excel. God planned that there be differences, unique capabilities, and variations in the church. So concerned was He that we realize this, He spelled it out several times in the New Testament. Take the time to read 1 Corinthians 12 *slowly* and *aloud*. Those thirty-one verses tell us about God's desires and designs—which are more attractive than thirty-one flavors!

The subject is commonly called "spiritual gifts," and it is as helpful as any truth that believers can ever know, perhaps more. In a nutshell, here's the scoop:

1. God has placed us in His family and given each of us a certain mixture that makes us unique. No mixture is insignificant!

2. That mix pleases Him completely. Nobody else is exactly like we are. That should bring us pleasure too.

3. When we operate in our realm of capabilities, we will excel and the whole body of Christ will benefit . . . and we will experience incredible satisfaction.

4. When others operate in their realm, balance, unity, and health automatically occur in the body. It's amazing!

5. But when we compare . . . or force . . . or entertain expectations that reach beyond our or others' God-given capabilities, mediocrity or total defeat is predictable.

So let's relax and accept how God made us. Let's cultivate our capabilities and stop comparing ourselves to others. Enjoy being unique!

25

God's Holiness, Our Need

SING PRAISE TO THE LORD, YOU HIS GODLY ONES, AND
GIVE THANKS TO HIS HOLY NAME. —PSALM 30:4

———————— ✥ ————————

WE COME BEFORE YOU, *our Father, and we acknowledge that
it is Your holiness that draws us to You. And it is that lack of holiness
in ourselves that brings from within us such a hunger to know You
better. We affirm with Paul that our determined purpose is that we
may know You. That we may progressively become more intimately
acquainted with You. God, that is what we want. More important,
that is what we need.*

*In a culture that's adrift and in a world that's broken, there is
something about Your character that guides us and restores us. Your
holiness warms our hearts and breaks our stubborn wills. And we
stand before You, our holy God, acknowledging that You are pristine,
free of corruption, without a hint of sin or transgression.*

We are reproved by Your command: "Be holy, for I am holy." The angels acknowledge You by saying, "Holy, holy, holy is the Lord God, the Almighty." You are high and lifted up. You have full perspective and understanding. Your character is unflawed, and we are lost in the wonder of it. We are caught up in the perfection of Your person.

We've never known a Father like You, as good as our fathers may have been. We've never known One so full of compassion and grace and love and mercy. Introduce us again to who You are. Remind us of it again and again, especially when we fail and see ourselves so unworthy. Remind us that none of that blocks Your wondrous forgiveness. Thank You. Thank You.

In the matchless name of Jesus, Your Son and our Savior, we pray. Amen.

See Isaiah 6:1–7; Romans 12:1; Ephesians 1:3–4; Philippians
3:10; 1 Peter 1:14–16; Revelation 4:8.

OUR INCOMPREHENSIBLE GOD

Lost in the silent solitude of recent days, I have been impressed anew with the vastness of our incomprehensible God.

I find His incomprehensibility absolutely refreshing, especially in a day like ours where managerial moguls prance like peacocks and deified athletes strut their stuff. At a time when one-upmanship and human intimidation have become an art form, it is delightful to be reminded anew that our God is the Lord. He is the maker of heaven and earth. He is the Lord . . . the Maker of heaven and earth, the Alpha and the Omega, the sovereign God of the entire universe.

And what are the benefits of such a realization? We stop reducing God to manageable terms. We are no longer tempted to manipulate Him or His Word. We don't have to explain Him and His will or defend Him and His ways.

In a world consumed with thoughts of itself, filled with people impressed with each other, having disconnected with the only Holy One worthy of praise, we need to catch a glimpse of Him who alone is awesome, yea, *incomprehensible*. He is our infinite, inexhaustible God. Any serious study of Him takes us to conscious awareness of our ignorance. The One we worship defies human analysis.

Let's discipline ourselves to think on these things, refocusing our minds from the horizontal to the vertical. May we rise above the nonsense of human viewpoint and tedious worries about temporal issues and get on with thoughts that really matter. Then let's stay there.

It's time we got reacquainted with our Maker.

26

Christ's Life, Our Clarity

HE DIED FOR ALL, SO THAT THEY WHO LIVE MIGHT NO
LONGER LIVE FOR THEMSELVES, BUT FOR HIM WHO DIED AND
ROSE AGAIN ON THEIR BEHALF. —2 CORINTHIANS 5:15

O LORD GOD, YOU HAVE NOT LEFT US *to wade through murky waters of uncertainty or to wander in a fog of confusion. Rather, because Your Son lives, we have a clarifying perspective on our lives. There is something about Christ's life that flows like lava beneath the crust of our daily living. How valuable His life is to ours! We fall back on it over and over.*

We remain grateful, dear Father, that the risen Savior conquered not only sin and the grave, but also disease and death. His death vanquished sin . . . and His resurrection conquered death. Drawing on the strength of His life causes us to find delight in living our lives. Help us to think straight even though the culture around us has lost its way, believing that right is wrong . . . and wrong is right.

Realign our thoughts, our Father, to the clarifying truth of Jesus' life,

death, and resurrection.

Direct our steps in these difficult days. Remind us of our Savior,

who conquered the grave, turning tragedy into triumph. We live and

we pray in the name of the risen Savior, Jesus Christ. Amen.

See also John 13:15; Romans 6:4–5; 14:7–9; 1 Peter 2:21.

BEING REAL

Every once in a while, some hotshot athlete walks away from his team and responsibilities, muttering the familiar remark, "I need to get my head together." Typically, team management, players, sportscasters, and fans are puzzled as to what he's looking for. But I'm not.

He is searching for that sense of purpose and inner fulfillment that his sport and all its benefits cannot provide. It's like an inner itch that can't be scratched by achievement or even a huge fan base. To "find yourself" requires that you take the time to look. It's essential if you want to be a whole person, real to the core.

Now I'm not advocating that we suddenly stop everything to work through the hide-and-seek process. That's rather unrealistic. Learning to be real isn't prompted by copping out. But there are times in life when we need to back off, slow down, stay quiet, think through, be still.

"But I'd rather burn out than rust out!" shouts the zealot. Frankly, neither one sounds very appealing to me. Either way you're "out." There *has* to be more to life than just doing. There is! It's *being*. It's becoming whole . . . believable . . . purposeful . . . lovable. The word is *real*. It takes time. And it's a process—always lengthy, often painful.

And it never happens apart from Jesus. Never.

Take a long look at *you*. In a hurry most of the time? Seldom pausing to ask why? Still reluctant to be real? You cannot play cover-up forever.

Let's drop our guard and get real. God wants us to have a heart of compassion, being kind, tender, transparent, gentle, patient, forgiving, loving, and lovable. All those things spell R-E-A-L.

27

Cultivating Life Change

THE SEED IN THE GOOD SOIL, THESE ARE THE ONES WHO HAVE
HEARD THE WORD IN AN HONEST AND GOOD HEART, AND HOLD
IT FAST, AND BEAR FRUIT WITH PERSEVERANCE. —LUKE 8:15

———————— ﻌﺞ ————————

PLOW UP THE SOIL *of our souls, our Father, as You walk through the garden gate of our hearts. Plant life-changing seeds of Your truth into the creases of our minds. Replace our poor, longstanding habits with better attitudes and clearer thoughts. Cultivate our hearts to receive an understanding of Your Word. We long to enter into what this process of life change really means—the sacrifice, surrender, and submission that lead to obedience. Instead of uprooting our weeds by means of guilt, I pray that a realization of Your grace will refresh us like soft-falling rain of renewed hope—the hope of being different than we've ever been . . . of looking at life from a new perspective . . . of experiencing inner growth that has never been there before.*

Our Father, today we surrender to You our hearts, our ambitions, our treasure, our dreams, our plans—all of who we are and what we do. Instead of these being mere words, may they be the beginning of something magnificent. May we discover a deep and abiding joy as we surrender our lives to Your cultivation of our souls. In the name of Jesus, we pray. Amen.

See also Isaiah 58:11; Luke 10:27; John 15:1–11; Romans 12:1–2.

AN ALTERNATIVE GAME PLAN

Going through tough times these days? Tempted to hang it up if things don't change? Wondering why more folks don't rally around your flag? I understand, believe me. Let me suggest an alternative game plan that I picked up from King David during one of his most difficult tests.

Israel had won a victory, but David had lost his son in the process. Before the two of them could make things right, the rebellious Absalom was suddenly killed. The grief that gripped David can be fully understood best only by those who have lost a son or daughter. Try to imagine the moment immediately after David got the news.

His mourning immobilized the grieving king, causing the heroes of the war to return without the king's welcome. Like many of America's veterans of Vietnam, the Hebrew soldiers received no honor upon returning home. The king's grief eclipsed the nation's victory. David's general, Joab, reproved David for his shortsightedness. Joab pulled no punches, saying that if David didn't affirm those who fought for him, they would soon turn against him (2 Samuel 19:5–7).

To David's credit, he listened. God had called him to rule as a model of unselfishness before the people, his loss notwithstanding. David grasped a broader perspective and found sufficient strength to go on in spite of great grief. Choking back his tears, he returned to his tasks and the nation rejoiced. So must you and I. But how?

Here's the alternative game plan: *we press on by realizing that our greater calling is of higher priority than our personal pain.* You *can* go on . . . you really can. Trust me. It will take extra effort, no question about it. It will call for more than a little faith and courage. Surrender your life to God's game plan . . . and then press on.

28

God as Supreme Ruler

His dominion is an everlasting dominion which
will not pass away; and His kingdom is one which
will not be destroyed. —Daniel 7:14

WE LIFT UP OUR VOICES, *our Father, in gratitude for Your
role as Supreme Ruler over our lives. Thank You for giving us life at
conception, breath at our birth, and love in our family. For many of
us, our upbringing shaped our convictions and habits—those principles that led to lives we would never otherwise have known. Thank
You for Your compassion, for caring for us with such fatherly love and
understanding. We're grateful for Your tenderness, for being there to
comfort us in the depths of our grief and to encourage us in the height
of our celebrations.*

*We give You praise for the magnificent power You provide which
we would not otherwise have. For enlightening us with an understanding of the Holy Scriptures. For illuminating our minds to grasp*

such insightful information. For delivering divine truth designed to give us light and life . . . and for freeing us from the shackles of religion and the shame of legalism.

Your sovereign hand directs us to a life of mercy and fills our hearts with beautiful music, adding the grace notes that touch us in moments we least expect them—but most need them. In the majestic name of Your Son, we bow before Your supreme dominion. Amen.

See also Job 14:5; Psalm 139:16; Daniel 4:34.

WHATEVER HE PLEASES

When the bitter news of Dawson Trotman's drowning reached the shoreline of Schroon Lake, panic struck. Eyewitnesses tell of the anxiety, the tears, the profound unbelief that swept across everyone's face. Everyone except one—Lila Trotman, Dawson's dear widow. As she walked upon the scene, someone shouted, "Oh, Lila, he's gone! Dawson's gone!" To that she replied in calm assurance with the words of Psalm 115:3: "Our God is in the heavens; He does whatever He pleases."

The anguish that normally consumes and cripples those who survive did not invade that woman's heart. Instead she leaned upon her sovereign Lord, who had once again done what He pleased.

Does that seem strange to you? Does it seem unusual to refer to a tragic death as being God's pleasure? Honestly now, do you think that God's control over us is total—or partial? Let's allow His Word to speak on this deep subject:

- "In Your book were all written the days that were ordained for me, when as yet there was not one of them" (Psalm 139:16).

- "Woe to the one who quarrels with his Maker—an earthenware vessel among the vessels of earth! Will the clay say to the potter, 'What are you doing?'" (Isaiah 45:9).

Pretty convincing words, if you ask me. And these are just two verses out of many in God's Word. Our Bible is literally filled with scriptures that parallel this same theme.

Lila Trotman bore the marks of spiritual maturity and faith as she faced the ways of God that were "unsearchable" and "unfathomable" (Romans 11:33).

29

Gratitude

THEREFORE AS YOU HAVE RECEIVED CHRIST JESUS THE
LORD, SO WALK IN HIM, HAVING BEEN FIRMLY ROOTED
AND NOW BEING BUILT UP IN HIM AND ESTABLISHED
IN YOUR FAITH, JUST AS YOU WERE INSTRUCTED, AND
OVERFLOWING WITH GRATITUDE. —COLOSSIANS 2:6–7

———————— ·~· ————————

YOU ARE INFINITELY HOLY, *our Father. It is beyond our ability to imagine someone so pure. You are good and gracious. You are full of kindness and love. Your mercy is perfectly balanced with Your justice—though we can't begin to fathom how. You cared about us when we didn't even care about ourselves. You sought us and saved us when we were sprinting in the other direction. You set the Hound of heaven after us . . . and You found us . . . and You won us over. Thank You. You gave the One who knew no sin to be sin, for us, and You transferred His righteousness to us. We who once were unworthy, filthy outcasts still find that hard to believe.*

We love, Father, because You first loved us. It is with hearts over-flowing with gratitude that we confess we are Yours and our lives are in Your hands. Your infinite mercy, grace, and kindness shown to us in Christ give us glimpses of Your infinite holiness. Our gratitude knows no bounds. In the name of Jesus, who makes intimacy with You possible, we thank You. Amen.

See also Luke 19:10; 2 Corinthians 5:21; Hebrews 12:28; 1 John 4:19.

ONE HUNDRED PERCENT

Remember that forgotten word *justification*? Here's my personal definition: "Justification is the sovereign act of God whereby He declares righteous the believing sinner while still in a sinning state." (Read that again, only slower.)

God doesn't *suddenly make* us righteous (we still sin); He *declares* us righteous. Two words stand out in that definition: "declares righteous." How righteous does God declare us? He declares us *100 percent* righteous.

When you consider how sinful, how totally depraved all of us really are, that fact is all the more remarkable. Stop and think: upon believing in Jesus Christ's substitutionary death and bodily resurrection, the once-lost sinner is instantly, unconditionally, and permanently declared 100 percent righteous. That means that in God's eyes He sees us from then on—positionally—as pure as His Son. Anything less and we are not righteous . . . we're *almost* righteous. Which means that if we were declared 99.9 percent righteous, Jesus' words to the thief on the cross wouldn't have been nearly so reassuring. It would have gone something like this: "Truly I say to you, at some time in the future, you might be with Me in Paradise . . . or, at least, let's hope so."

Nonsense! God's promise of sins forgiven is all or nothing at all. Eighty percent won't cut it . . . or 90 percent . . . or 99 and 44/100 percent . . . or 99.9 percent. Let's face it, 0.1 percent is still sinful. I mean, would you drink a gallon of water with only 0.1 percent of strychnine in it? Would you feel comfortable having a surgeon cut on you who was wearing *almost*-sterile gloves?

When our Lord said, "It is finished," He meant "finished." Because of that we're 100 percent justified.

30

Healthy Minds

THE MIND SET ON THE FLESH IS DEATH, BUT THE MIND
SET ON THE SPIRIT IS LIFE AND PEACE. —ROMANS 8:6

———————— ༄ ————————

ONLY YOU, OUR GOD, *can break the burdening bonds that
grip us. Release us so that we might enter into a realm of wellness—
spiritually, emotionally, and even physically. You will have to begin
that work within our minds, because we are incapable of pulling any
of this off by ourselves. Thank You that You do not dump us on this
earth and then leave us to do the best we can. You are no cold and distant deity. You lead Your dear children along. Though evil comes and
adversity strikes, You remain our God. You are never taken by surprise; You know the end, the beginning, and everything in between.*

*We pray You will help us leap beyond our daily mental distractions
so that Your Spirit enables us to apply what we read from Your Word.
May Your truth change our thoughts and, ultimately, our actions.*

We invite You, our Father—beginning at this moment—to take charge. Give us healthy minds, especially the ability to understand Your truth . . . that we may live it for Your glory. In the name of the One who is the truth, the way, and the life, we pray. Amen.

See also John 8:36, 14:18; Romans 12:1–2;
Philippians 1:6; Colossians 3:1–5; Hebrews 12:2.

THE MIND OF CHRIST

Periodically we will find ourselves at a loss to know what to do or how to respond. Life doles out those desperate times often, it seems. It's then we should ask for help. "If any of you lacks wisdom," James writes, "let him ask of God, who gives to all generously and without reproach, and it will be given to him" (1:5).

At those junctures when we need clear-thinking wisdom for times of trial, God delivers more than intelligence and ideas and good ol' common sense. He dips into His well of wisdom and allows us to drink deeply from His cup. I cannot fully describe the benefits of receiving the refreshment He provides, but among them would be perception and insights that are of another world. Perhaps it would best be stated as having a small portion of "the mind of Christ." To borrow from Paul, we are given: "Not . . . words taught by human wisdom, but . . . those taught by the Spirit, combining spiritual thoughts with spiritual words. . . . For who has known the mind of the Lord, that he will instruct Him? But we have the mind of Christ" (1 Corinthians 2:13, 16).

When we have responded as we should to life's blows, enduring them rather than escaping them, we are given more and more maturity that stays with us. God provides new measures of wisdom that we are able to draw upon for the balance of our lives.

If you're anything like I am, I have a sneaking suspicion that you could use some divine assistance to help you endure. If so, say so. Don't hesitate to call for help. Tell your Father that you are running out of hope and energy and ideas. Go ahead and admit that your mind is getting foggy and you need some fresh insights from the mind of Christ.

31

Indescribable

LIFT UP YOUR EYES ON HIGH AND SEE WHO HAS CREATED
THESE STARS, THE ONE WHO LEADS FORTH THEIR HOST
BY NUMBER, HE CALLS THEM ALL BY NAME; BECAUSE OF
THE GREATNESS OF HIS MIGHT AND THE STRENGTH OF HIS
POWER, NOT ONE OF THEM IS MISSING. —ISAIAH 40:26

OUR FATHER, WE OFTEN SEARCH *for words to describe our
gratitude for You. Certainly, we could begin with* profound, *for who
You are and for what You have done. Your power knows no bounds.
Another word is* deep, *for from the depths of our souls we pause on
occasion and marvel at Your character. To look up and realize that
the One who named the stars and put each one in place knows our
name, knows the number of our days, and even knows the number of
hairs on our heads. Our gratitude for You deepens with such realization.* Unique *is another word, our Father, for we have a gratitude*

for You as for no other. You are the one and only object of our affec-

tion. You are the one and only subject of our praise.

It all boils down to this: You are indescribable. *It's absolutely*

impossible for us to be able to express the inexpressible in words.

Therefore, because we haven't the words to say, we are content to

give You our lives afresh. May our love and obedience let You know

how profoundly and deeply and uniquely we worship and adore You.

In the indescribable name of Jesus, we pray. Amen.

See also 2 Samuel 7:18–21; Job 23:13; Isaiah 40:12–18; 2 Corinthians 9:15.

LET THE WONDER IN

It seems to me that if the Son of God found it necessary at the crossroads of His earthly existence to pray, "Not as I will, but as You will" (Matthew 26:39), we would be wise to use the same eight words often. Every day.

We need that reminder, we who are tempted to think we're capable of calling the shots. We need to be brought down to size, we who feel we've got a corner on our own destiny. How many times does God need to tell us that His ways are past finding out before we begin to believe it? How often must He prove to us that He is the

Shepherd and we are the sheep . . . that He is the Vine and we are the branches, before we bow and quietly whisper, "Have Your own way, Lord"? But not only do we feel capable of declaring His plan for our lives, we also think we have the ability to discern His panoramic plan across the board. *What a joke!* We're doing well to "trust and obey" on a day-to-day basis.

I'll be honest with you, the more I probe the outer limits of our universe—be it starry sky or stormy sea, majestic mountain or microscopic minutia—the more I want to be still and let the wonder in. What a wonder-full God we serve!

Such moments do what they're supposed to do: stir us so that an essential change takes place. God becomes what and who He should be to us, namely, indescribable—because He is unfathomable. Holy? Of course. Powerful? Yes, no question. Compassionate? Always. Righteous, gracious, loving, self-sufficient, sovereign? All the above, certainly.

But more . . . so much more. More than we can grasp. More than we can think. More than the brightest among us can even *imagine*.

32

Inerrancy

ALL SCRIPTURE IS INSPIRED BY GOD AND PROFITABLE FOR
TEACHING, FOR REPROOF, FOR CORRECTION, FOR TRAINING IN
RIGHTEOUSNESS; SO THAT THE MAN OF GOD MAY BE ADEQUATE,
EQUIPPED FOR EVERY GOOD WORK. —2 TIMOTHY 3:16–17

THANK YOU, O GOD, *for breathing out Your Word through the miracle of inspiration . . . and for preserving Your message in a Book we can read in our own language. Thank You for Your Word— the inerrant, authoritative, infallible Word of God. We live in a day where others' words have now replaced eternal Words. We pray that the scales will be lifted from their eyes and that which has blocked the hearing of Your truth will be removed so that they might see and hear and be comforted, encouraged, and transformed by the unchanging words of life. May the truth that appears in the Bible emerge as we read it. May it make its way through minds and into hearts, changing each of us so that our lives are imperceptibly conformed to the image of Jesus.*

Father, we pray that You will cause us to glean from Your Word truth to live by—and truth to die for. In this chaotic age, the battle for the souls of men and women, teens and children is one that rages in the mind. Transform us all, our Father, with your truth. "Your Word," Jesus prayed, "is truth." Open our minds to grasp the value of those great doctrines that anchor us to the bedrock of objective truth. In the name of the One who is called "the Word"—and for His glory—we pray. Amen.

See also Proverbs 30:5; John 1:1; 17:17; Romans 12:1–2; Hebrews 4:12; 2 Peter 1:19–21.

THE INFALLIBLE AND THE FALLIBLE

Ever since I was knee-high to a gnat, I have been taught and have believed in the infallibility of Scripture. We may fuss around with a few of the events in God's eschatological calendar or have differing opinions regarding church government. But when the subject turns to infallibility, the inerrancy of Holy Writ, there's no wobble room. Can't be. Take away that absolute and you've opened an unpluggable hole in your theological dike. Given enough time and pressure, it wouldn't be long before you and everything around you would get soggy and slippery. Make no mistake about it, the infallibility of Scripture is a watershed issue.

Infallibility is certainly true of the Bible, but it is not true of people. The Berean believers are commended for listening to Paul and then "examining the Scriptures daily to see whether these things were so" (Acts 17:11). It's easy to forget people aren't perfect, especially when we come across gifted people whose instruction is biblical, wise, and dynamic. Everything's great until one such individual teaches something that is different from another minister who is equally admired. That never fails to leave groupies in a confused tailspin. If I could change a term and put it in the language of Lincoln: all men are created fallible. Yes, all. If you remember that, you'll have fewer surprises and disappointments. Rather than slumping into cynicism because your hero showed feet of clay, you'll maintain a healthy and intelligent objectivity. You'll be able to show respect without worshiping. And when you really need to know the truth, you'll turn to the Scriptures with firsthand confidence.

Why? Because the Word of God is the only thing that's incapable of error . . . not ever to mislead, deceive, or disappoint.

33

Intercession

WE HAVE NOT CEASED TO PRAY FOR YOU AND TO ASK THAT
YOU MAY BE FILLED WITH THE KNOWLEDGE OF HIS WILL IN ALL
SPIRITUAL WISDOM AND UNDERSTANDING, SO THAT YOU WILL WALK
IN A MANNER WORTHY OF THE LORD. —COLOSSIANS 1:9–10

OUR FATHER, WE PRAY *on the behalf of others this day. There
are so many whose hearts are heavy. They live in lonely and painful places—and yet, they are in the nucleus of Your will. Some are
making Christ known in countries where that message is not per-
mitted. Their secret work must be done with great wisdom, through
keen strategy, and by careful planning. They face danger . . . but
they remain undaunted. Others have heavy hearts because they have
begun a new season of life without their loved one beside them. They
struggle with grief through long, dark nights. We also pray for those
who are experiencing their last year with those they love—and yet,*

they have no idea it is so. Help them to make the most of their time so that precious memories remain.

Encourage those who have lost their health and cannot come to the place of worship but would love to be able to enjoy the fellowship of the body of Christ. Thank You for those who serve You faithfully—all who serve their country in uniform, all who serve in the home with young children, all who serve in distant places who translate the Scriptures—all around this world in different time zones. Encourage all Your servants this day. We pray for them in the name of the magnificent Savior, whom they serve. Amen.

See also 1 Samuel 12:23; Isaiah 40:28–31; Colossians 1:9–12; 2 Thessalonians 1:11.

PRAYING FOR ONE ANOTHER

While reading through a section of 1 Samuel, I ran across a passage of Scripture that illustrates graphically the value—the essential importance—of our praying for others.

Here's the scoop. Samuel is in the thick of it. His nation is going through a tough, uncertain transitional period. They have pressed for a king and gotten their way. It fell to Samuel's lot to confront them . . . to spell out the lack of wisdom in their stubborn urgency to be like all the other nations. They saw the foolishness in their decision after the fact (isn't that usually the way it is?). On top of their guilt, they witnessed the Lord's sending thunder and rain that same day, which only intensified their fears.

What next? How could they go on, having blown it so royally? Wisely, they made the right request of Samuel: "Pray for your servants . . . for we have added to all our sins this evil by asking for ourselves a king" (1 Samuel 12:19).

Greathearted Samuel must have smiled as he reassured them: "Far be it from me that I should sin against the LORD by ceasing to pray for you" (12:23). He had already been praying for them, so he promised not to stop. To do so would be a sin against the Lord.

I call that important.

There is no more significant way we can be involved in another's life than prevailing prayer, consistent prayer. It is more helpful than a gift of money, more encouraging than a strong sermon, more effective than a compliment, and more reassuring than a warm embrace.

Far be it from us that we should sin against the Lord by ceasing to pray for one another.

<u>34</u>

It Is Well

"For My thoughts are not your thoughts, nor are your ways My ways," declares the Lord. "For as the heavens are higher than the earth, so are My ways higher than your ways and My thoughts than your thoughts." —Isaiah 55:8–9

———————— ༒ ————————

WE SING THE GREAT HYMN *"It Is Well," Father, but truth be told, it is not always well with our souls. Often we find ourselves troubled to the point where we cannot sleep. Some days we hope against hope. We find ourselves so shocked on occasion that, were it not for the truth You have revealed to us, it would appear You've lost control. But that could never be. It's just that Your plan is filled with mystery. And even though our lives are marked by inexplicable and illogical events, somehow, in some remarkable manner, they are all unfolding exactly as You have designed.*

We ask that it might be well with the souls of those who are deeply troubled and anguished today. May the compassion of Your great heart somehow find its way into the minds and thoughts of those who have lost hope. Remind us, Lord, that life is tenuous and ever so brief—like a vapor that appears for a little while and then vanishes. Use times like this to prepare us that we might say with all our hearts, "It is well with my soul." In the name of the only One who understands our times and comforts our souls, even Jesus, we pray. Amen.

See also Romans 4:18; 11:33–36; James 4:14.

MORE LIFE IN YOUR DAYS

After a memorial service for a friend who died with liver cancer, I thought about how to respond when struck by an arrow of affliction. Not a little irritating dart, but an arrow plunged deeply into the vitals.

My friend chose not to curl up in a corner with a calendar and put Xs on days as they passed by. On the contrary, the news only pressed him to squeeze every drop out of every day. His physician told him he'd probably be gone before Thanksgiving. "Says who?" he replied. Not only did he live through Thanksgiving, but at Christmas he threw a party, the following Easter was delightful, a fun picnic on the Fourth of July was a blast, and he had a special cele-bration in the planning stage for *the following* Thanksgiving. I even heard he made an appointment to have his teeth fixed! That kind of spunk underscores one of my philosophies of life: *when struck by an arrow, don't seek more days in your life but more life in your days.* Forget quantity. Start shooting for quality. If we look beyond the pain we'll find incredible perspective. Arrows don't change our direction. They merely deepen our character.

So which arrow has struck you recently? News of a so-called ter-minal illness? Physical pain? Unfair treatment? False accusations? Struggles at home? I encourage you not to waste time licking your wounds or wondering why. Make a decision to do what you were doing even better than ever. Remember now: *don't seek more days in your life but more life in your days.*

Arrows are nothing more than momentary setbacks that help us regroup, renew, and reload—so let's get on with it. We could even get our teeth fixed!

35

Leading

HE LEADS ME BESIDE QUIET WATERS. HE RESTORES MY
SOUL; HE GUIDES ME IN THE PATHS OF RIGHTEOUSNESS
FOR HIS NAME'S SAKE. —PSALM 23:2–3

———————— ༕ ————————

ON THIS NEW DAY, OUR FATHER, *we acknowledge Your
leading in all of our lives. You led in our birth. You chose the time,
the place, and our parents. You chose us to be reared in that home,
and You led us through each day of our childhood. You faithfully
stayed with us through the turbulent teenage years that followed. As
we grew and got serious about spiritual things, You brought us to
a knowledge of Your Son, Jesus, and caused us to realize that there
is hope in Him that can be found in no other name. How grateful
we are that You enabled us to understand the good news of Christ's
death, resurrection, and offer of eternal life by faith alone—in Christ
alone—through Your grace alone.*

Thank You for leading us in the years that have followed to this very day. We have been guided by the wisdom of the Spirit of God. Not knowing what the future holds, we invite You to lead on, O King Eternal. Lead on! Remind us over and over that we do not walk alone, nor dare we walk our own way.

In the magnificent name of our Savior, Master, Leader, and Lord, Christ, we pray. Amen.

See also Psalm 5:8; 31:3; 71:6, 17; 129:1–2; Isaiah 48:17; John 6:44.

WHEREVER HE LEADS

Abraham faced the challenge of following God into the unknown when he pulled up roots from his hometown, Ur, and split for—let's see, where *was* he going? He didn't know!

There he was, almost seventy-five years old, loading up a camel caravan with his wife and family, bound for . . . *somewhere*. Hebrews 11:8 says it straight: "By faith Abraham, when he was called, obeyed by going out . . . not knowing where he was going."

That's like a competent Christian businessman I know who left a secure, six-figure position to enter a whole new career without training or expertise in the field . . . who, after he learns the ropes, may

(I repeat, *may*) gross a mere twenty thousand dollars if things fall together.

"Why are you doing this?" I asked him.

With incredible assurance he answered, "One word—*God*." I've seldom seen a person more confident, more fulfilled.

Are you on the verge of such a decision? Is the Lord loosening your tent pegs, suggesting it's time you take a drastic leap of faith— counting on Him to direct your steps through a future that offers no tangible map? Great! But before you jump, be sure of four things:

- Be sure it's the Lord who is leading.
- Be sure the decision doesn't contradict Scripture.
- Be sure your motive is unselfish and pure.
- Be sure the "leap" won't injure others or your testimony.

It's helpful to remember what God calls us: "strangers and pilgrims" (Hebrews 11:13 KJV). People on the move, living in tents, free and unencumbered, loose and available, ready to roll, willing to break the mold—whenever and wherever He leads. Regardless.

36

Our Guide

FIXING OUR EYES ON JESUS, THE AUTHOR AND PERFECTER
OF FAITH, WHO FOR THE JOY SET BEFORE HIM ENDURED THE
CROSS, DESPISING THE SHAME, AND HAS SAT DOWN AT THE
RIGHT HAND OF THE THRONE OF GOD. —HEBREWS 12:2

WE HAVE YOU, OUR FATHER, as our God and Your Son as
our Guide. You remind us to turn our attention from where we are
. . . to where we're going. Thank You for pointing the way emphati-
cally and clearly and in a manner we will not easily forget. How
grateful we are that You preserve Your truth in a book that is time-
less, ageless, priceless, and true.

Lift our hearts above where we find ourselves today—above all
the distractions that could break us into a sweat. Keep our eyes fixed
on Jesus—the author and perfecter of faith—and bring us back to the
reliable voice of God, as found in the print on the pages of Your Word.
Remind us, whenever we glance at the cross, what it means to live

sacrificially, as Your Son lived on our behalf. May Your blessing rest upon our lives, which we offer up to You. Fill us with anticipation, remembering that our best days are yet to come.

We give You praise, our God, for the pleasure You bring to us . . . and for the joy set before us. In the name of Jesus, whom we love, we pray. Amen.

See also Philippians 3:20; 1 Thessalonians 1:10.

REASONS TO FOLLOW

Okay, let me guess. Your life is full of appointments, activities, and a few aggravations—right? If so, you may be looking for your significance in your own achievements.

After reading Luke's account of the miraculous catch (Luke 5:1–11), I want to suggest four reasons we should stop forcing our own agendas and instead start following the Master's. Each reason could be stated in a principle.

Jesus moves us from the safety of the seen to the risks of the unseen. Nothing significant occurred in shallow water. He specifically led the disciples "out into the deep water" where nobody could touch bottom (Luke 5:4). The deep is always full of uncertainties, but that's the realm God prefers. That's where God does His best work.

Jesus proves the potential by breaking our nets and filling our boats. Not one of those weary fishermen would've bet one denarius that there were so many fish in that lake! When God's hand is on a situation, nets break, eyes bulge, deck planks groan, boats lean—and hearts change. It's His way of putting the potential on display.

Jesus conceals His surprises until we follow His leading. Everything was business as usual on the surface. Those fishing boats didn't have a halo, nets didn't tingle at their touch, the lake water didn't glow. No. The divinely arranged surprise came only after they dropped the nets.

Jesus reveals His objective to those who release their security. He could read their willingness in their faces. Then (and only then) did He tell them they'd be engaged in "catching men" (v. 10). And guess what—they ultimately jumped at the chance!

You may find it helpful, on occasion, to take this mental boat trip out into the deep. It will transform your agenda from one you're forcing to one you're following.

37

Our Part in God's Plan

ALL THE INHABITANTS OF THE EARTH ARE ACCOUNTED AS NOTHING,
BUT HE DOES ACCORDING TO HIS WILL IN THE HOST OF HEAVEN
AND AMONG THE INHABITANTS OF EARTH. —DANIEL 4:35

⁓

WE ACKNOWLEDGE THAT YOU ARE *in Your heaven, our Father, and You are accomplishing whatever is according to Your will on this earth. Yet even though all the inhabitants of the earth are accounted as nothing You have commanded us to obey You, and You expect us to be people of prayer.*

Our God, remind us that while You are at work, we, too, are engaged in the fulfillment of Your plan. Not one of us is designed by You to be passive, uninvolved, indifferent, or complacent in the work of ministry. What a tempting message from the enemy! May it be silenced forever in our minds and ignored in our wills. May we be those who turn to You often for strength. May we faithfully tell others about Your Son, Jesus. Use us mightily to declare Your truth.

Stir us up from within, our Father, as we realize that time is short . . . and that days are full of emptiness and heartache, as well as discouragement and depression. Help us to become praying people who pour out our hearts to You with passion. In the name of the Savior, who gave us the Great Commission, we pray. Amen.

See also 1 Samuel 12:23; Isaiah 40:17: 41:11–12; Daniel 4:35; Matthew 28:18–20; Luke 18:1; 1 Thessalonians 5:17; 2 Peter 1:13: 3:1.

GUTSY CHRISTIANITY

The name was Bonhoeffer. He was one who refused to shrug his shoulders, smile sweetly, and keep quiet about what was wrong. As a result, he was arrested and imprisoned on April 5, 1943. For two years he remained imprisoned by the Nazis.

On Easter Sunday, April 8, 1945, this unique servant of God preached his final sermon from prison. It consisted of a simple service of worship, a text: "With His Stripes We Are Healed," a prayer, and a few tears. Suddenly, the door bolted open—"Prisoner Bonhoeffer, come with us." A brief good-bye followed. He pulled one man aside and whispered, "This is the end, but for me it is the beginning of life."

In the gray dawn of the following morning, in the concentration camp at Flossenburg, the beloved Dietrich Bonhoeffer was hanged on the gallows by special order of Heinrich Himmler. It seems a cruel irony that his execution occurred only days before the Allied forces arrived and liberated the camp. But who can question the length of one's life if God is truly sovereign? Perhaps his death did more to underscore his memory than a long life ever could.

In a day like ours when shallow thinking, superficial faith, and secret-service saints litter the landscape, it is reassuring to call to mind a name that became a synonym for gutsy Christianity. The next time you're hesitant to stand alone or to speak out in defense of the truth, even though doing so may be misunderstood, remember that name. It belonged to one for whom God was real and always near . . . one of those "men of whom the world was not worthy" (Hebrews 11:38). The man is gone, but his name and his words endure.

The name was Bonhoeffer.

38

Our Vision

THE LORD WAS GOING BEFORE THEM IN A PILLAR OF CLOUD
BY DAY TO LEAD THEM ON THE WAY, AND IN A PILLAR OF
FIRE BY NIGHT TO GIVE THEM LIGHT, THAT THEY MIGHT
TRAVEL BY DAY AND BY NIGHT. —EXODUS 13:21

BE TO US WHAT WE CAN NEVER BE *for ourselves, our Father. Be our vision. We're grateful that You take us into life's journey without our knowing on the front end where that journey will lead. We only have a glimmer of an understanding . . . and it's often complicated. In a world that's chaotic, disturbing, and often disillusioning, there are details that have not been addressed. Admittedly, we have more questions than answers. But that's where You come in.*

We invite You to invade our inner space. Be our vision. Be our guide while life shall last. Bring understanding, insight, and courage. In a world of demanding deadlines, unforgiving spirits, and revengeful people, open our hearts where we have been rigid and reluctant. May we live with the great encouragement that our Savior died for us, never holding against us what we have done against Him. Be our vision. It's so easy for us to be shortsighted and afraid of tomorrow, insecure today, or worried over yesterday. May You find in our lives of love and obedience the tangible proof of our gratitude to the One who is our life, our hope, our vision. We pray in the name of Jesus, our Savior. Amen.

See also Exodus 13:21; 14:19; Psalm 77:19; 78:52; 80:1; Isaiah 63:11–13.

SEEING BEYOND THE PRESENT

David and his fellow warriors were returning from battle. Exhausted, lonely, dirty, and anxious to get home, they came upon a scene that took their breath away. What was once their own, quiet village was now a black heap of smoldering ruins. On top of that, the enemy forces had kidnapped their wives and children. David and his men wept until they could weep no more (1 Samuel 30:4–5). And if that were not bad enough, David's own men turned against him. Talk of mutiny swirled among the soldiers.

If ever a man felt like hanging it up, David did at that moment. But he didn't. What did he do instead? Read this carefully: "But

David strengthened himself in the LORD his God" (1 Samuel 30:6). He poured out his heart before the Lord and got things squared away vertically. All that helped clear away the fog horizontally. How did he go on? *He refused to focus on the present situation only.*

What happens when we stay riveted to the present misery? One of two things: either we blame someone (which makes us bitter) or we submerge in self-pity (which paralyzes us). I'm reminded of Paul's words to the Christians in Rome: "I consider that the sufferings of this present time are not worthy to be compared with the glory that is to be revealed to us" (Romans 8:18). Going on with our lives will never occur as long as we concentrate all our attention on our present pain.

David found himself unable to escape tough times. What is so encouraging is that he determined not to stay there. He picked up the pieces, got his act together, held his head high, drew strength from his Lord, and pressed on. If he could do it, so can we.

39

Parenting

FROM CHILDHOOD YOU HAVE KNOWN THE SACRED WRITINGS WHICH
ARE ABLE TO GIVE YOU THE WISDOM THAT LEADS TO SALVATION
THROUGH FAITH WHICH IS IN CHRIST JESUS. —2 TIMOTHY 3:15

———————— ৺ ————————

FATHER, FORGIVE US *for getting so caught up in the rapid life-*
style of this century that we neglect our own children. Slow us down
long enough to remember days gone by. You were the One who chose
us to be reared by our parents. Those who loved us poured their lives
into us . . . prayed for us . . . and formed in their minds what we
would be today. Thank You for our parents. What good models they
were to provide us with such great memories. We thank You for them,
even though each was far from perfect.

Father, please grant all parents, stepparents, and foster parents
a sense of destiny. Help us recognize the significant role You have set
aside for us to fill, which no one else can play. Erase from our minds
all the paraphernalia and cultural nonsense that would attempt to

persuade us otherwise. Convince us of the value of being a parent—a

servant of the living God.

We pray that as a result of our lives, there will be a difference made in a world that is now unhinged. May we be increasingly more committed to our responsibilities. As our children grow up, may we as parents change from instructors to mentors . . . and ultimately, to friends. In the name of Jesus, we pray. Amen.

See also Genesis 18:19; Deuteronomy 6:7; 11:19; Psalm 78:4; Proverbs 22:6; Ephesians 6:4; 2 Timothy 1:15.

HOLDING CHILDREN LOOSELY

Shortly before her death, Corrie ten Boom attended the church I pastored. Following one worship service I met briefly with her, eager to express my wife's and my love and respect for her example. She soon inquired about my family and our children. She detected my deep love for each child, which bordered dangerously near too much love. Cupping her wrinkled hands in front of me, she passed on a statement of advice I'll never forget. I can still recall that strong Dutch accent: "Pastor Svindole, you must learn to hold everyting loosely. Everyting. Even your dear family. Why? Because da Fater may vish to take vun of tem back to Himself, und ven He does, it vill hurt you if He must pry your fingers loose." And then, having tightened her hands together while saying all that, she slowly opened them and kindly smiled as she added, "Vemember, hold everyting loosely. *Everyting*."

That was our last conversation. As I watched her walk away, I thought of Corrie losing her sister Betsy in the Ravensbrück Nazi death camp, no doubt her darkest hour. It was probably then God taught her the principle she relayed to me so many years ago.

Now that we have raised our children—and we find ourselves wanting to cling to our ten grandchildren—Cynthia and I will occasionally repeat Corrie's counsel to each other, "Vemember . . . hold everyting loosely."

We all would be wise to start practicing that seasoned wisdom. Whatever we have that means more to us than it should, or whomever we love too much and therefore clutch too tightly, let's release to God's care. "Vemember . . . hold everyting loosely. *Everyting*."

40

Patriotism

HONOR ALL PEOPLE, LOVE THE BROTHERHOOD, FEAR
GOD, HONOR THE KING. —1 PETER 2:17

———————— ୬ ————————

OUR FATHER, HOW GRATEFUL WE ARE *for our liberty!*
Thank You for our nation. Though it is far from perfect, how mag-
nificent to call it our home. Give us an appropriate sense of pride in
our land and for our flag. Help us to model a national loyalty in such
a way that the younger generation grasps what it means to be patri-
otic. We owe a special measure of gratitude to You for the devotion
of those who fell in battle, whose crosses line vast areas here in our
homeland and abroad, marking those places where they once fought
. . . and died. Thank You for each courageous warrior.

While we love our country and find special delight in being free,
our adoration is not directed to this land, but to You, our Father.
May our love for country in no way conflict with our reverence for

Christ. We would have no other gods before You. We confess that no other name is higher, no other Savior is Lord, no other god is Creator, no other One is worthy of our worship. To You we pledge our utmost allegiance, to You and You alone. Out of worship and gratitude, we pray in the name of the One who is ours—and who died to make us free indeed—even Christ. Amen.

See also Exodus 20:3; John 8:36; 15:13; 1 Corinthians 7:21–22; 1 Peter 1:1; 2:11.

SPIRITUAL LIBERTY IS YOURS

I think it's strange that we Christians are reluctant to allow ourselves to do . . . to think . . . or to be different—and not worry about who may say what. Funny, even though our God has graciously granted us permission to be free, many in His family seldom give themselves permission.

They have strange reasoning: "I mean, after all, what would people say?" or "Well, I was taught to be more conservative than that." So goes the persuasion of an oversensitive conscience trained in the school of negativism. Tragic. Worse than that, it is downright unbiblical. Just last evening I read, "Where the Spirit of the Lord is, there is liberty" (2 Corinthians 3:17). Let that word sink in. *Liberty.*

In other words, enjoy! Be who you are. Give yourself the okay to break the mold and exercise your God-given freedom. I don't mean you can become a jerk. I'm saying you may have to train yourself to care less and less about what a few may say.

Until we all give ourselves permission to be the unique people God made us to be and to do the unpredictable things His grace allows us to do, we will continue to march in vicious circles of fear, timidity, and boredom. God, in grace, has purchased us from bondage. Christ has literally set us free. The Spirit of the Lord has provided long-awaited liberty.

Since the strings have been cut, it's time for us to stop marching and start flying. Let's give ourselves permission to lift our wings and feel the exhilaration of a soaring lifestyle. Grace frees us to fly. So, let's fly!

41

Prodigals

QUICKLY BRING OUT THE BEST ROBE AND PUT IT ON HIM, AND
PUT A RING ON HIS HAND AND SANDALS ON HIS FEET; . . . FOR
THIS SON OF MINE WAS DEAD AND HAS COME TO LIFE AGAIN;
HE WAS LOST AND HAS BEEN FOUND. —LUKE 15:22, 24

OUR GOD AND FATHER, *we pray for those who are rebels on
the run . . . wayward prodigals who, at this very moment, are distant
from You. We ask that You would draw them to Yourself as only You
can do. The parable our Savior told of the prodigal and his father is
as timeless as it is true. What a stirring reminder it is, our Father, of
all of us in our earthly journey. It isn't difficult for us to identify with
this boy! We've all been there more often than we care to remember.*

*We pray, God, for every father and mother whose hearts are
breaking over a rebellious child. We ask You to bring their son or
daughter back to their senses. We pray that You would develop the
children into godly men and women. Cause us to realize what You*

can do in the life of any individual who is wholly dedicated to You. Bring repentance, encouragement, and relief to those prodigals—and great hope to families who love them—who, this very day, are broken and bruised and bewildered. In the name of Jesus our Savior, we pray. Amen.

See also Isaiah 53:6; Luke 15:1–32; John 6:44; 1 Thessalonians 5:14.

COMPASSION WAITS

The timing is as critical as the involvement. We don't just force our way in. Even if we've got the stuff that's needed, even if our piece is perfectly shaped to fit the other person's missing part of the puzzle . . . we can't push it into place. We must not try. We must do the most difficult thing for compassion to do. We must wait.

Yes, that's correct. *Wait.*

Even if there is rebellion? Yes, even if there's rebellion. *Wait.*

Even if sin is occurring? Yes, often even then. *Wait.*

Even if others are suffering and disillusioned and going through the misery of misunderstanding, heartache, sleepless nights? Believe it or not, yes. There are times (not always, but often) when the better part of wisdom restrains us from barging in and trying to make someone accept our help. The time isn't right, so we wait.

Like Isaiah reported to the nation, whom the Lord called "rebellious children" (30:1). There were shameful deeds, reproachful behavior, unfaithful alliances, oppression, and a ruthless rejection of God's Word. Their unwillingness to repent added insult to injury. But what do we read of the Lord's response? Hidden away in the first part of verse 18 is the incredible statement: "Therefore the LORD longs to be gracious to you, and therefore He waits on high to have compassion on you."

Instead of storming into the dark alleys of Judah, screaming "Repent!" and shining bright floodlights to expose the filthy litter of their disobedience, the Lord tapped His foot, folded His arms ... and waited. The time wasn't right.

Not even the Lord pushed His way in. So ... why should we?

42

Reflection

REMEMBER THAT YOU WERE AT THAT TIME SEPARATE FROM
CHRIST, EXCLUDED FROM THE COMMONWEALTH OF ISRAEL,
AND STRANGERS TO THE COVENANTS OF PROMISE, HAVING NO
HOPE AND WITHOUT GOD IN THE WORLD. —EPHESIANS 2:12

*OCCASIONALLY, OUR LORD, WE NEED to reflect and
remember. We need moments when we remember and reaffirm Your
sovereignty. Your Word proclaims that you are in the heavens, and
You do whatever You please. That is as it should be. You are the
Potter; we are the clay. You are the Master; we are the servants. You
are infinite; we are finite. You never waver; we often waffle.*

*We need these days to reflect on Your goodness, even though we
don't deserve it. As we reflect, we repent. How shallow is our commitment . . . how short-lived is our determination. While we do not
deserve Your goodness, You continue to lavish it upon us. Thank You*

for giving us what we do not deserve, for placing Your favor on us who are stubborn and often disobedient. Find in us today ears open to hear, eyes anxious to see, and wills ready to obey. May our lives represent true gratitude for Your sovereignty, Your goodness, Your mercy, and Your grace. Through Christ, we pray. Amen.

See also Exodus 13:3; Psalm 115:3; Isaiah 64:8; Ephesians 2:11–12; Revelation 2:5.

A WARM HEART

The delicious aroma of charbroiled T-bones drifted through the rooms. The ladies laughed in the kitchen as they prepared the meal. The easy, relaxing atmosphere made you want to kick off your shoes in front of the crackling fireplace.

A friend of mine leaned his broad shoulders against the mantel as he told of the bass that got away. My eyes ran a horizontal path across the carved message on the mantel. The room was too dark to read it from where I sat. I was intrigued and strangely drawn from my overstuffed chair to get a closer look.

I ran my fingers through the outline of each letter as my lips silently formed the words: "If your heart is cold, my fire cannot warm it."

How true, I thought. Fireplaces don't warm hearts. Neither does fine furniture, nor a four-car garage, nor a six-figure salary. No, only the fire of the living God can warm a cold heart.

I settled back down, stayed quiet, and prayed as I stared into the fire: "Lord, keep my heart warm. Stop me when I move too quickly toward stuff I think will make me happy. Guard me from this stupid tendency to substitute things for You."

The dinner bell broke the spell and I stood up. I took a quick backward glance to remind myself of the words one more time: "If your heart is cold, my fire cannot warm it." I thanked God for His fire that has never burned down.

That memorable scene occurred decades ago now. My heart has, since then, occasionally cooled off. Today, however, it is warm because He never left me when I was cold.

43

Resting in Silence

Therefore humble yourselves under the mighty
hand of God, that He may exalt you at the
proper time, casting all your anxiety on Him,
because He cares for you. —1 Peter 5:6–7

———————— ༄ ————————

WE ARE STRANGERS TO MANY THINGS, *our Father, but most of all to silence. We find ourselves so busily engaged in life that we hate to miss even one panel of a revolving door. We dash to work . . . we rush through the day . . . we choke down our lunch . . . we speed through each afternoon . . . and we hurry home. Our activity is constant. Rarely—if ever—do we deliberately slow down . . . sit in silence . . . and let the wonder in. Help us to do that right now. May we rest in You in the quietness of this moment. May we be still and learn anew that You are God.*

We cast our cares on You. We release our struggles and place them on Your shoulders. We give our worried hearts to You. We rest in knowing You command a multitude of capable angels to watch over us, Your children, because You love us. We rest in the knowledge that Your Spirit empowers us to live a life that is beyond our own ability. Our victory reflects Your power, not ours. That strips away all the pride, all the strain, all the self-effort. You free us to rest in the joy of who You are. We thank You for all these things in the name of Jesus, who is our rest. Amen.

See also Psalm 37:7; 46:10; 55:22; Matthew 6:25.

AN EASY YOKE

Left to ourselves, we'll opt for extremes virtually every time. That explains why God's Word so often addresses moderation and self-control, softening our sharp-cornered lives with more curves that necessitate a slower speed.

The psalmist counsels us to "cease striving" so we can know that God is God (Psalm 46:10). Even Jesus found it necessary to get away on occasion just to be alone. And who can forget His gracious invitation? "Come to Me, all who are weary and heavy-laden, and I will give you rest. Take My yoke upon you and learn from Me, for I am gentle and humble in heart, and you will find rest for your souls. For My yoke is easy and My burden is light" (Matthew 11:28–30).

In our high-tech day of high-level pressures, Jesus offers us rest. Twice in one statement. While so many others are demanding, He's gentle. While competition is fierce and being in partnership with hard-charging, bullish leaders is tough, being yoked with Him is easy. Yes, easy. Instead of increasing our load of anxiety, He promises to make it lighter. Is it any wonder Jesus' style and message created such a stir? While so many were piling on more guilt, more "shoulds" and "musts," He quietly offered relief.

So, let me ask *you*, where do you go to find enough stillness to rediscover that God is God? Where do you find rest when your days and nights start running together? What spot becomes your hideaway so that a little perspective is gleaned and a little sanity returns? How do you get relief from the fever-pitch extremes?

These are questions only you can answer. And because only you can ... *please do*.

44

Saying Yes

HE SAID TO THEM, "FOLLOW ME, AND I WILL MAKE
YOU FISHERS OF MEN." IMMEDIATELY THEY LEFT THEIR
NETS AND FOLLOWED HIM. —MATTHEW 4:19–20

———————— ༄ ————————

OUR FATHER, YOU COMMANDED US *to follow Jesus, and
we said yes. Thank You, Lord, for Your command. We are on that
journey, so we count on Your patience with us as we follow Your Son.
We are learning that most are journeys we would never have imag-
ined ourselves. We have seen You open surprising doors and pave the
way for ministries we could never have envisioned back when we
first said yes.*

*Oh, Lord, what a privilege life with You has been! How faithful
You are! May our yes continue to ring in our ears and hearts. May
we look for further reasons to say yes to You. May we always respond
to Your leading with yes on our lips.*

Hear us, our Father, even now when we face today's challenges.

Our answer is still a resounding "Yes!" We will follow You willingly because we trust You implicitly. Perhaps our journeys occur for no other reason than to declare how great it has been to walk with You. We commit our lives to You with an enormous yes written across our minds.

We pray in the name of Jesus, who Himself said yes to a rescue mission that no one else could have accomplished. Amen.

See also Luke 9:23; John 21:19; 2 Corinthians 1:17–20.

EVERYTHING

No one can criticize Peter for being reluctant. He'd been fishing all night and caught zilch. But when Jesus told him, "Put out into the deep water and let down your nets for a catch," Peter wisely thought, *Okay.* What happened was nothing short of miraculous (Luke 5:4–7). Their haul was so huge both boats, filled with fish, began to sink!

Since I love to fish, I find that scene terribly inviting. Can anything be more satisfying to a fisherman than standing hip-deep in fish? I have never seen that occur! That's because I have never fished with Jesus.

When the Master of heaven, earth, sea, and skies calls the shots, phenomenal things happen. That explains Peter's reaction. Gripped with the realization that he was in the boat with the living God, Peter fell facedown in the fish at Jesus' feet, and said, "Go away from me Lord, for I am a sinful man!" (v. 8).

I find Jesus' reply a little surprising: "Do not fear, from now on you will be catching men" (v. 10). The fish were merely an opportunity to teach a deeper message by analogy. Jesus' real message was "catching" people. Furthermore, Jesus uses people to catch people— even though He could do it alone. Jesus didn't sail the boats, throw the nets, or haul in the catch. *The disciples did.* In His message, Jesus stated, "From now on you will be catching men." Peter and the other fishermen connected the dots. That's why they "left everything" (v. 11) and followed Jesus.

Once they heard His words, they accepted His invitation. They dropped everything and said yes. Ponder "everything." Their lifelong occupation. Their familiar surroundings. Their own goals. Their nets, boats, and successful fishing business. *Everything.*

No hesitation. No reservation. No condition. They left everything.

45

The Lord of All Seasons

He did not leave Himself without witness, in that He did good and gave you rains from heaven and fruitful seasons, satisfying your hearts with food and gladness. —Acts 14:17

In the quietness of this moment, *our Father, we acknowledge that You are the Lord of the seasons. You change them during the cycle of each year, and yet You remain changeless. You alone, as Creator, are the God of all nature—there is no Mother Nature. You, alone, shape the natural world around us. You are not only our Creator, but You are our Father through faith in Your Son, Christ Jesus.*

We come as Your children, dear Father, to thank You for Your hand of grace on our lives, Your mercy for us in our need, and Your understanding of us just as we are. As we pause to enjoy the seasonal changes, we also pause to dedicate our lives to You afresh and anew. We thank You for the joy that comes in knowing the Savior, having

Him as our advocate and friend—the One who is interceding for us,

loving us, caring about us, and meeting our needs.

By Your grace, our Father, You give us comfort and guidance in

these changing seasons. Yet there really is nothing we can give You

that You need . . . except to affirm that we dedicate ourselves to You.

This day is Yours, O Lord . . . this season is Yours . . . our hearts are

Yours. Through Christ our Savior, we pray. Amen.

See also Daniel 2:21; Hebrews 13:8; James 1:17.

———————— ✑ ————————

THE DESIGN AND THE DESIGNER

Let's remind ourselves of a few fundamental, proven facts of science we learned in high school. All of these relate to the planet we're standing on.

All of earth's heat is from the sun, which is 12,000 degrees Fahrenheit. We are ninety-three million miles away—just the right distance, I might add. If the earth's temperature were an *average* of 50 degrees hotter or colder, all life on this planet would cease to exist. Why is the sun 12,000 degrees? Why not 1,200 degrees, or 120,000, or 24,000? Why was the earth fixed at *exactly* the right distance away so that we can have pleasant temperatures in the fall and spring—

and yet not too extreme for the summer and winter? I'll tell you why: because all life would perish. Our oxygen constitutes about 21 percent of our atmosphere. Why not 4 percent or 10 percent or, for that matter, 50 percent? Well, if it were *50* percent, the first time someone lit a match we'd *all* be on fire.

My point? God designed this planet so that it would support one thing: life. Without life, earth would be another planetary wasteland. It would be like a wedding without a bride . . . or a car without gears and wheels. Why life? Because only through life can creatures like us understand God and glorify our Maker! Only through faith in the Lord Jesus Christ can the designed know and glorify the Designer.

If you are making no attempt to know and glorify your Creator, that kind of life has definite consequences and a fixed destiny. Pause and ponder that horrible destiny . . . lasting separation from your Designer.

Science can observe the design—the sun and the seasons—but only through eyes of faith can we see the Designer. Are you looking?

46

Spiritual Healing

[IF] MY PEOPLE WHO ARE CALLED BY MY NAME HUMBLE
THEMSELVES AND PRAY AND SEEK MY FACE AND TURN FROM THEIR
WICKED WAYS, THEN I WILL HEAR FROM HEAVEN, WILL FORGIVE
THEIR SIN AND WILL HEAL THEIR LAND. —2 CHRONICLES 7:14

IF THERE HAS EVER BEEN *a land that needed healing, Lord,
it is ours. We have fallen upon hard times. Our homes need healing
because our families are fractured. Parents distant from children . . .
siblings no longer talking with each other . . . children estranged from
parents . . . marriages ending in violence . . . children abused and
abandoned. We see brokenness at every turn.*

*We also need healing in our churches, our Father. Denomina-
tional infighting and mudslinging. A church on one corner refusing
to speak to people in the church on another. The splits are more than
we can keep up with. People are deeply offended, held hostage by hard*

feelings, unforgiveness, bitterness, and blame. All sin—*at the core of*

every unresolved conflict.

Hear our prayer, our Father, as we pause, humble ourselves, and

seek Your face. Halt the erosion. Prompt us to turn from our wicked

ways, that we might hear from heaven, and You might forgive our

sins and heal our land. Begin with each one of us, and accomplish this

spiritual healing from the inside out. We pray in the name of the only

One who can heal us—even Jesus. Amen.

See also 2 Chronicles 7:14; Jeremiah 18:7–10; James 4:10; 1 Peter 5:6.

FRIENDSHIP

F riendship is a sheltering tree," wrote Samuel Taylor Coleridge. How very true! When the searing rays of adversity's sun burn their way into our day, there's nothing quite like a sheltering tree—a true friend—to give us relief in its cool shade.

I remember the trees in Paul's life that significantly sustained him. Barnabas stood by him when everyone else ran from him (Acts 9:26–27; 11:25–26). There was Silas, his traveling companion over many a lonely mile (Acts 15:40–41). When you add Dr. Luke, Timothy,

Onesiphorus, Epaphroditus, and Aquila and Priscilla, you find a veritable *forest* of sheltering trees surrounding that great man's life.

Beneath whose branches are you refreshed, my friend? Or, I could ask, who rests beneath *yours*? Occasionally, I run across an independent soul who shuns the idea that he or she needs such shelter, feeling that trees are for the immature, the spiritual babes . . . those who haven't learned to trust only in the Lord. It is *that* person I most pity, because his or her horizontal contacts are invariably superficial and shallow. Worst of all, their closing years on earth will be spent in the loneliest spot imaginable.

Let's be busy about the business of watering and pruning and cultivating our trees, shall we? Would I be more accurate if I added *planting* a few? Cultivating friendships takes time. You will really need a few sheltering trees when the heat rises and the winds begin to blow.

But I should remind you that a real, genuine, deep, solid friend is exceedingly rare. Either you're still looking through the forest . . . or, like me (thank God), you're enjoying shade and shelter today beside a few, very special God-given trees.

47

The Crucible

NOW FOR A LITTLE WHILE, IF NECESSARY, YOU HAVE BEEN
DISTRESSED BY VARIOUS TRIALS, SO THAT THE PROOF OF YOUR
FAITH . . . MAY BE FOUND TO RESULT IN PRAISE AND GLORY AND
HONOR AT THE REVELATION OF JESUS CHRIST. —1 PETER 1:6–7

FATHER IN HEAVEN, AS DIFFICULT *as it is to endure, we
thank You for how You transform us in the crucible of pain. You challenge our fears, invade our resentments, change our habits, and crush
our pride. These crucible moments fall so hard upon us that it seems
You are ruining our lives. Help us understand, our Father, it is just
the opposite. You are renovating our whole inner person, not simply
by the suffering of our flesh but by the breaking of our wills. Indeed,
our Father, You are very much alive and completely involved in our
lives during these painful experiences.*

*We ask that as You crush us, reduce us, break us, and mold us, that
You will find in us hearts receptive to Your will. By Your grace, on*

occasion, please reveal to us the reasons for the crucible—those new depths of insight and the new dimensions of spiritual life that only suffering can bring.

We're grateful that You are shaping us into the image of Your Son, who prayed in Gethsemane, "Not my will, but Yours be done." We pray in the name of our magnificent Savior, who, though Your Son, learned obedience through the things He suffered. Amen.

See also Luke 22:42; James 1:12–13; 1 Peter 4:12–13; Hebrews 5:8.

THE ARDUOUS ROAD TO MATURITY

One day as I was having lunch with a successful businessman, the subject of wisdom kept popping into our conversation. At one point, I asked him, "How does a person get wisdom? I realize we are to be men of wisdom, but few people ever talk about how it is acquired."

His answer was quick and to the point: "Pain."

I paused and looked deeply into his eyes. Without knowing the specifics, I knew his one-word answer was not theoretical. He and pain had gotten to know each other quite well. After listening to the things he had been dealing with in recent months, I told him he had spent sufficient hours in the crucible to have earned his PhD in wisdom! While sitting there with him, I was prompted to quote from the first chapter of James in the Phillips paraphrase of the New Testament:

> When all kinds of trials and temptations crowd into your lives my brothers, don't resent them as intruders, but welcome them as friends! Realise that they come to test your faith and to produce in you the quality of endurance. But let the process go on until that endurance is fully developed, and you will find you have become men of mature character with the right sort of independence. (vv. 2–4)

Aren't those great words? More importantly, they are absolutely true. By accepting life's tests and temptations as friends, by allowing them to wade into our private world to produce the rare quality of endurance, we become people "of mature character." There is no shortcut, no such thing as *instant endurance*. The pain brought on by interruptions and disappointments, by loss and failure, by accidents and disease, is the long and arduous road to maturity, which leads on to wisdom. There is no other road.

48

The Whys of Life

O LORD, MY HEART IS NOT PROUD, NOR MY EYES HAUGHTY;
NOR DO I INVOLVE MYSELF IN GREAT MATTERS, OR IN
THINGS TOO DIFFICULT FOR ME. —PSALM 131:1

AS WE SEARCH OUR HEARTS TODAY, *our Father, we acknowledge there are many more things we don't understand than those things we do. We confess we don't know the reasons You have put us together as You have. We can't explain our temperaments, tastes, or our trials. We don't understand our tempers or our times. Our moods are often so strong they control our minds and actions. We have no idea what tomorrow holds . . . or next year . . . not even the next hour. We don't know how long we will live or how we will die. As the psalmist writes, these things are too difficult for us.*

More disturbing than the puzzling facts and events are the reasons they occur. The whys of life are, far too often, more important to us than they should be. Why was our loved one taken? Why have our lives been marked by this present course? Why have we known such blessing and favor this year? How could You be so gracious to ones so undeserving?

Dear Lord, help us to not involve ourselves in such matters too difficult for us. We admit that although we cannot explain the whys of life, we believe You do all things well. Confessing that You alone are our sovereign God, we leave these things in Your hands. Through Christ, we pray. Amen.

See also Psalm 88:14; 90:12; 131:1; Proverbs 3:5–6; 27:1.

GOD IS STILL SOVEREIGN

King David was cornered on the heels of a rebellious insurrection. Rather than stand against the plot of a civil war, David abdicated and fled with his loyal followers. That alone must have been humiliating, but what followed added insult to injury.

A man named Shimei took the opportunity to curse the king. Keeping a safe distance, Shimei ran parallel with David's demoralized crew and hurled stones as well as accusations (2 Samuel 16:5–8, 13). Nice guy, huh? We can count on it: there will always be a Shimei who kicks us when we're in a helpless position, while sharing a piece of his mind he can't afford to lose.

One of David's colleagues named Abishai asked permission to put Shimei out of his misery. "I'll slit his throat so fast he won't know it 'til he sneezes!" (Swindoll paraphrase). The king restrained him with incredibly wise words: "Let him alone and let him curse, for the LORD has told him. Perhaps the LORD will look on my affliction and return good to me instead of his cursing this day" (2 Samuel 16:11–12).

Sound theology won the day! Instead of retaliating or curling up in a corner and licking his wounds, David called to mind that not even this event was a mistake. The Lord wasn't absent. On the contrary, He was in full control. David faced the test head-on and refused to throw in the sponge. How did he do it? *By remembering that God is still sovereign.*

Few doctrines have brought me greater comfort than this one. When I cannot understand why, God is sovereign. When the events absolutely defy my own logic, God is sovereign. And even when the pain intensifies because some Shimei jumps in with a handful of stones and takes a few unfair shots, God is *still* sovereign.

49

Timeless

HE CHOSE US IN HIM BEFORE THE FOUNDATION
OF THE WORLD, THAT WE WOULD BE HOLY AND
BLAMELESS BEFORE HIM. —EPHESIANS 1:4

———————— ﭪ ————————

HOW GRATEFUL WE ARE, *our Father, that You are not restricted by time. With You, there is no Tuesday or Friday . . . no morning or evening . . . no last week or next week . . . no yesterday or tomorrow. With You there is only eternal now. You are in full control of all that will transpire this day or any day. You know what the past has included. You know what the future holds. Truth be told, You've known these things even before the foundations of the world were in place.*

Father, thank You for life and the gifts life brings. The gift of time. The joy of past and present relationships. The pleasure of building memories that last. We pray that as we grow older we will become wiser. May we learn to keep Your eternal truth close to our hearts, that we might be better women and men in this present world while we await the next one.

Whether our days are many or few, and whether Your Son comes in our generation or not, we commit our lives to You. May each and every day be well spent, meaningful, memorable, and all for Your glory. In the name of Jesus, we pray. Amen.

See also Psalm 90:12; Ecclesiastes 3:11; John 17:24; James 1:17; 1 Peter 1:20.

A WISE USE OF TIME

We have a wonderful gift of sixteen waking hours every day. Yet when all is said and done, and some undertaker finally closes the lid on our coffin, here are the facts. The average American's lifetime includes: *six months* waiting at stoplights, *eight months* opening junk mail, *a year and a half* looking for lost stuff, and *five years* standing in lines. *I knew it!* I was sure that hidden in the cracks lay an unbelievable number of hours.

Since there is no way we're going to escape from all the stupid time-traps that accompany existence, seems to me we're left with two choices. Either we can whine about the six months at stoplights or we can take the time we have and spend it wisely. I mean *really* wisely with our priorities in the right order.

And speaking of that, what are you doing with the rest of your life? I'm talking about the deliberate pursuit of meaningful activities that will yield eternal dividends. Do you have a family? Rather than leaving them the leftovers as you give your job your best hours and your most creative ideas, how about rethinking the value of strengthening those ties? And while we're at it, let's not leave out necessary time for quietness with God, for personal refreshment beside a rippling stream, for watching a sunset, for deep worship at dawn. And don't miss some stimulating exercise—a swim in a lake, volleyball with friends under a warm afternoon sun, maybe an early morning jog or walk fueled by clean air for a change.

Does it seem like you don't have time to add anything else to your squirrel-cage lifestyle? Look closely, and you'll find all kinds of time hidden in the cracks.

50

Wholeness

NOW MAY THE GOD OF PEACE HIMSELF SANCTIFY YOU
ENTIRELY; AND MAY YOUR SPIRIT AND SOUL AND BODY BE
PRESERVED COMPLETE, WITHOUT BLAME AT THE COMING
OF OUR LORD JESUS CHRIST. —1 THESSALONIANS 5:23

—————————— ب —————————

OUR DEAR FATHER, WE DESIRE *that every part of our lives be whole and wholesome. We long for physical health for our friends, our family, and ourselves. We request that You do what You alone can do: bring healing to our bodies, minds, and souls. Doctors prescribe . . . but You heal. We long to have sound minds, so that one thought follows another in a logical and appropriate manner. Help us make decisions that are wise. Give us unswerving courage and conviction to stand for what we know is right in a world that has drifted far from You. We long to be emotionally well and able to endure the hammer blows of affliction. Even when we are misunderstood or maligned, give us the determination to press on. We ask for emotional wellness so that we might have relationships that are truthful and intimate, not hypocritical or insecure.*

Most of all, our Father, we ask for health in our souls. Deep within us—where only the scalpel of Your razor-sharp Word is able to pierce the soul and spirit—may we become well. May we no longer pursue those things that are bad for us, but follow You and You alone.

In the name of the only One who can make us well, we pray. Amen.

See also Deuteronomy 6:5; Mark 12:30; Luke 2:52; 3 John 2.

A TRIUMPHANT SPIRIT

Cancer. The very word has a hiss in it. When the doctor uses the term, you immediately churn, your heart is chilled, your head swims. You tell your family and a few close friends and then you begin a process of believing the unbelievable. Words like "incurable" and "terminal" and "treatments" and "*whatever* therapy" crowd out all other thoughts as you lie awake at night. For the first time in your life, you feel mortal. Prayer is no longer a theological theory.

Even though your body is carrying a disease, you are determined not to let it conquer your mind. Good for you! Your health may go through some severe ups and downs, but your spirit can become triumphant. You want that more than anything else this side of a miraculous healing . . . so what can you do? You tell God you have an emergency need: "I have cancer, Lord, and I need wisdom on a daily basis." At that moment He will begin to make His deliveries. And each morning from then on you accept the gift of His wisdom in the Bible and count on His strength for that day. You quickly discover that your greatest enemy is not the disease but subtle, slippery feelings of despair, the thief of peace. You decide to rely on God's daily delivery service to get you through that one day. And then the next. And the next.

You may ultimately be healed. You may not. Whichever God sovereignly wills will be your lot. But in the meantime, you can be transformed into a whole person of mature character.

51

Living on Tiptoe

BY FAITH ABRAHAM, WHEN HE WAS CALLED, OBEYED
BY GOING OUT TO A PLACE WHICH HE WAS TO RECEIVE
FOR AN INHERITANCE; AND HE WENT OUT, NOT KNOWING
WHERE HE WAS GOING. —HEBREWS 11:8

———————— ༄ ————————

OUR FATHER, TEACH US *what it means to live on tiptoe. To
trust You when we do not know what the future holds . . . when the
destination is unclear . . . when Your plan has not yet run its course.
Remind us, our Father, that You are pleased when we walk by faith
. . . and grieved when we walk by sight.*

*We acknowledge that You often direct our paths to places unknown
to us. You are a God of surprises, although nothing surprises You—
for You, O Lord, know it all. You know our thoughts before we think
them . . . our heartaches before we suffer them . . . our dreams before
we dream them. Our lives are unfolding and we are living them
from one day to the next, not knowing what a day will bring forth.*

You are carrying out Your perfect plan. You are relentlessly at work within us.

We pray that You will guard us from exasperation while we live in expectation. Silence our fear. Take away all temptation to panic. Remove the wrestling and the anxiety connected with trials that often enter our lives and sometimes stay. Remind us that even there, You are acquainted with all our ways. In the strong name of Jesus our Savior, we pray. Amen.

See also Psalm 5:8; 77:19–20; 139:3; Acts 20:22.

OUR SERENDIPITOUS SAVIOR

Though I have walked with God for many decades, I must confess I still find much about Him incomprehensible and mysterious. But this much I know: *He delights in surprising us.* He dots our pilgrimage from earth to heaven with amazing serendipities we never expected. Serendipity occurs when something serenely beautiful breaks into the monotonous and the mundane. A serendipitous life is marked by surprisability. When we lose our capacity to be surprised, we settle into deep, dull ruts. We expect little and we're seldom disappointed. A serendipitous life is also distinguished by spontaneity . . . the ability to spot and seize the unexpected and then respond with delight to the unplanned. Few things bring back our smile more quickly!

How important it is for us to remain sensitive and open. There are insights to be discovered which the Spirit of God quietly whispers. There are solutions to be applied, profound lessons to be learned, unexpected scenes to be enjoyed, surprising discoveries to be made. The hurried and irritable soul misses them.

Isaiah's words make me smile every time I read them: "Behold, I will do something new, now it will spring forth; will you not be aware of it? I will even make a roadway in the wilderness, rivers in the desert" (43:19). Your situation may be as hot and barren as a desert or as forlorn and bleak as a wasteland. You may be tempted to think, *There's no way!* when someone suggests things could change. I encourage you to read that verse one more time. Does God lie? Are you an exception?

Since our serendipitous Savior has been doing "something new" in places like drab deserts and wintry wastelands for centuries, I suggest you be on the lookout.

52

Forgive Our Trespasses

OPEN SHAME BELONGS TO US, O LORD, TO OUR KINGS,
OUR PRINCES AND OUR FATHERS, BECAUSE WE HAVE SINNED
AGAINST YOU. TO THE LORD OUR GOD BELONG COMPASSION
AND FORGIVENESS, FOR WE HAVE REBELLED AGAINST HIM;
NOR HAVE WE OBEYED THE VOICE OF THE LORD OUR GOD,
TO WALK IN HIS TEACHINGS WHICH HE SET BEFORE US
THROUGH HIS SERVANTS THE PROPHETS. —DANIEL 9:8–10

FORGIVE US, OUR FATHER, *for being attracted to the pleasures of sin . . . to what appears to be full of ecstasy and satisfaction but is, in fact, empty and stupid. Thank You for bringing conviction, for pointing out our rebellion. We need that reminder every day, so that we might invest ourselves in that which endures. We want to pursue the things of God, the things You consider important and valuable—a righteous walk, a pure heart, a committed lifestyle. We long to place family above fortune and purpose above fame and righteousness above riches.*

Our Father, You instruct us and teach us in the way we should go. Thank You for that. You shine a bright light on our path from Your Word. Thank You for the relief that comes with being forgiven and the peace of mind that accompanies a clean heart. Finally, thank You for Your mercies, new every morning, and Your grace, needed every day.

We thank You in the dear name of Jesus. Amen.

See also Matthew 6:12; Acts 10:43; Ephesians 1:7; Hebrews 9:22.

CALLING SIN *SIN*

A bomb exploded years ago in mid-America, of all places. The brainchild of this explosion was *the* Karl Menninger, MD—a name synonymous with the science and practice of psychiatry. That physician, that respected, competent pioneer of the profession actually had the gall to reintroduce the word *sin* to the nation's vocabulary. His book *Whatever Became of Sin?* stunned and shocked his colleagues.

All had been relatively quiet on the Western front. Eastern too. We were still licking our wounds from the street riots, campus rebellions, and political assassinations of the 1960s. We were biting the bullet of a prolonged war in Southeast Asia . . . and whistling in the dark through the threatening streets of Israel. Most of us sensed trouble was brewing . . . *something* was wrong. But none dared call a spade a spade. Certainly not *sin*. Horrors! How old-fashioned can you get! Once Menninger was gutsy enough to declare it, more and more people began to toy with the possibility . . . and some got their act together. A few are now even willing to admit (*hang on*) that mankind is depraved!

Reminds me of the apocryphal story of two parties of Native American Indians in the desert of New Mexico talking to each other by means of smoke signals. Suddenly a huge column of smoke appeared and began to climb rapidly some twenty miles into the air. Neither tribe had ever seen such a sight, nor had the world. It was exactly 5:30 a.m., July 16, 1945—the first atomic bomb test. One Indian leaned over to another, shook his head, and commented, "Wow! I wish I had said that!"

Menninger lit the fuse years ago. May his tribe increase.

53

Overcoming Guilt by Remembering Whose We Are

FOR I AM CONVINCED THAT NEITHER DEATH, NOR LIFE, NOR ANGELS, NOR PRINCIPALITIES, NOR THINGS PRESENT, NOR THINGS TO COME, NOR POWERS, NOR HEIGHT, NOR DEPTH, NOR ANY OTHER CREATED THING, WILL BE ABLE TO SEPARATE US FROM THE LOVE OF GOD, WHICH IS IN CHRIST JESUS OUR LORD. —ROMANS 8:38–39

GRACIOUS FATHER, *we're our own worst enemy. We focus on our failures rather than on Your rescues. We remember our wrongs rather than rejoice in Your power to make us right. We rely on our puny efforts to get through the day rather than on Your sovereign plans for our good. Even our attempts at being devoted to You are often self-centered and self-serving. Turn our attention back to You.*

Remind us of our exalted position in Christ—that You have qualified us to share in the inheritance of the saints in Light. Keep uppermost in our minds that You have rescued us from the domain of darkness and transferred us to the kingdom of Your beloved Son.

Refresh us with frequent flashbacks from Your inerrant and reliable Word: "If God is for us, who is against us?" "Who will separate us from the love of Christ? Will tribulation, or distress, or persecution, or famine, or nakedness, or peril, or sword?" "But in all these things we overwhelmingly conquer through Him who loved us."

Renew our spirits with the realization that we're Your possession—we are a chosen race, a royal priesthood, a holy nation, a people for Your own possession.

Then, with those joyful thoughts to spur us on, slay the dragon of guilt within us so we might enjoy Your comforting and reassuring embrace. Through Christ our conquering Savior, we pray. Amen.

See also Psalm 51:10; Romans 8:31, 35,37; Colossians 1:12–13; 1 Peter 2:9.

RIGHT THINKING

Consider your mind a factory . . . a busy, bustling place of action and production, for so it is! It produces thousands, perhaps *hundreds* of thousands, of thoughts each day. Production in your thought factory is under the charge of two foremen. One we shall call Mr. Triumph and the other Mr. Defeat. Mr. Triumph is in charge of manufacturing positive, wholesome, encouraging, reassuring thoughts. Defeat is responsible for the manufacturing of negative, depreciating, worrisome thoughts. Both foremen are instantly obedient. They await your signal to snap to attention. Provide yourself with a positive signal and Mr. Triumph will see to it that one encouraging, edifying thought after another will fill your mind. He will take life by the throat and refuse to let even the slightest cloud of doubt float overhead. But Mr. Defeat awaits a negative signal and he will crank out discouraging thoughts so that before long you are convinced that you *can't* or *won't* or *shouldn't*.

Our thoughts, positive or negative, grow stronger when fertilized with repetition. That may explain why so many who are gloomy stay that way . . . and why the cheery people continue to be so. Happiness is a matter of right thinking.

We need only one foreman in our mental factory. Mr. Triumph is anxious to assist us—he is available to all the members of God's family. His real name is the Holy Spirit, the divine Helper.

If Mr. Defeat is busily engaged as foreman of your factory, *fire yours and hire ours!* You will be amazed at how smoothly your busy, productive plant will run under His leadership.

54

Waiting

HE HAS MADE EVERYTHING BEAUTIFUL IN ITS TIME.
HE HAS ALSO SET ETERNITY IN THE HUMAN HEART;
YET NO ONE CAN FATHOM WHAT GOD HAS DONE FROM
BEGINNING TO END. —ECCLESIASTES 3:11–12 NIV

------------ ‿ ------------

THANK YOU, OUR FATHER, *for granting us the patience to wait on You. Many have been in Your waiting room for months; a few of us have been waiting for years. We ask that You will do a genuine work in our hearts during this waiting period. Develop within us a depth of character, an understanding of Your wisdom, and a peace in Your perfect will. In the mystery of Your plan, we place ourselves at Your disposal. We ask that You would freely work within each of us for Your greater glory. Whether Your will is that we continue to wait . . . or move forward, we will not question Your leadership.*

As we linger, our Father, remind us that You keep Your word and that Your promises are sure—for You are a God of integrity and veracity. We pray that You will give us fortitude while we're in this waiting room. As we live in expectation, may we learn that You do just what You say, but only and always in Your time. These things we ask in the magnificent name of Jesus, who is the same yesterday, today, and forever. Amen.

See also Psalm 27:14; 37:7; Isaiah 40:31.

BACK OFF AND GIVE GOD ROOM

Solomon, the wise, has given us a list of various "appointed times" on earth. Here are a few examples: "a time to heal . . . a time to shun embracing . . . a time to give up as lost . . . a time to be silent" (Ecclesiastes 3:3, 5, 6, 7). I see in his counsel one main thought: *Back off!* On many occasions, we need to relax our intensity, not force an issue, and allow nature to take its course. That provides "a time" for healing to occur.

When the time is right, things flow very naturally. To rush or force creates uncomfortable friction. How often we're like the little boy who plants the seed then nervously digs it up every day to see if it's growing. Waiting is as necessary as planting and harvesting.

You can't get sap out of a hoe handle. Nor can a relationship be corrected by legislation and force. That means being silent and allowing God to work. In other words, *back off* so the Lord can move in and take charge. This is a difficult pill for intense people to swallow. Kept edgy by impatience and strong determination, they continually and foolishly rush in. Guys can do this with the young women they date. She wants room to breathe, but he continues to smother. We can do this with individuals we have offended. They need time to think and freedom to forgive without being hurried.

Stop and think. Are you being wise or foolish? Are you using force or providing freedom? Are you being pushy or patient? Are you intimidating by your intensity . . . or backing off and relaxing?

Take it from one who is starting to learn this valuable lesson. It's always best to back off and give God room.

55

Living Life to the Fullest

CONDUCT YOURSELVES WITH WISDOM TOWARD OUTSIDERS, MAKING
THE MOST OF THE OPPORTUNITY. LET YOUR SPEECH ALWAYS BE WITH
GRACE, AS THOUGH SEASONED WITH SALT, SO THAT YOU WILL KNOW
HOW YOU SHOULD RESPOND TO EACH PERSON. —COLOSSIANS 4:5–6

———————— ﹏ ————————

OUR DESIRE, FATHER, *is to be fully present—all there—*
wherever we are. We want to live to the hilt every situation we
believe to be Your will. You have placed us in the twenty-first cen-
tury, with our specific families, in our particular neighborhoods.
May we live here, now, fully, completely, passionately. In our occu-
pations, may we fulfill wholeheartedly our calling. You have given
us the joy of the fellowship of the saints in a local church. May we
make the most of every opportunity to welcome others into it.

Lord God, deliver the body of Christ from becoming a museum
full of aging memories—dusty, dull, irrelevant, and out of touch. At
the same time, keep us attached to our past—to the great truths of

Your timeless Word and to the great music of the ages. In all of this, may we stay in touch with our world today. The needs are enormous and numerous. Help us know how to build bridges across the moat that separates us from a needy world, so that we become a point of comfort and authenticity, a place of hope, a harbor of relief, and rescue for those who have lost their way. In Jesus' name, we pray. Amen.

See also Psalm 31:23–24; 119:1–2; Proverbs 3:5–6; Matthew 22:36–39.

IT'S YOUR ATTITUDE
THAT MATTERS

As you begin to age, there are four attitudes that will demoralize you—as well as those who have to be around you. The first attitude is *uselessness*. This attitude says, "I'm over the hill. I just get in everybody's way." Uselessness causes you to die before you die. The German poet, Johann Goethe, was right when he wrote, "A useless life is an early death." The second attitude is *self-pity*. Self-pity says, "Nobody cares about me anymore. Why should I bother to stay alive? Woe is me." Invariably this leads to blame . . . which leads to bitterness . . . which leads your family to ask, "How long is Grandma visiting this time?" Don't misunderstand. Your family loves you . . . they just hate your self-pity. The third attitude is *fear*. This outlook says, "I need to be very careful. I need to avoid all dangers and all risks." Common among those getting older, a fearful attitude can quickly lead to a suspicious, paranoid spirit.

Fear is a thief that steals your joy and robs your peace. I believe it is one of the most devastating of all emotions. If you're afraid, chances are good you'll draw your blinds and double-lock your door . . . and you'll also miss most of the fun in life.

Perhaps the most devastating of the four is the attitude of *guilt mixed with regret*. This attitude forever looks back with a sigh: "If only I *hadn't* . . . If only I *had* . . ." Guilt and regret feed disappointment and discouragement. But God's grace removes our guilt and gives us a reason to press on.

Let's be honest. Do we see ourselves in any of these attitudes? If so . . . it's time for a major attitude adjustment. Start today.

56

The Importance of Prayer

O LORD, I BESEECH YOU, MAY YOUR EAR BE ATTENTIVE TO THE
PRAYER OF YOUR SERVANT AND THE PRAYER OF YOUR SERVANTS
WHO DELIGHT TO REVERE YOUR NAME. —NEHEMIAH 1:11

———————— ༄ ————————

FATHER IN HEAVEN, WE CALL *upon You today. We know
that You are the Giver of all good things . . . and that You never
change. Your heart is moved when Your people pray. So remind us,
our Father, that there is nothing more important we can do when
facing situations that are beyond us . . . than to pray.*

*We remember that prayer forces us to wait, and we must learn to
wait patiently for Your timing. Prayer quiets our hearts before You.
The chaos subsides and life seems to settle down around us as we pray.
Prayer clears our vision, Father, as we think about our lives, as we
ponder where we're going, and as we pursue Your will. May we walk
with You in such a way that our obedience is revealed through deeds*

that honor Your name . . . even when that means doing the hard things You want us to do.

For those who are under pressure, up against a wall, facing a test—we ask that You remind them that the saint who advances on his or her knees never retreats. Help them remember You are still on Your throne and they are still at Your footstool . . . with only a knee's distance between the two of you.

May we all become people who pray. May we also learn to leave the burden with You, rather than pick it up and carry it with us after claiming that we're trusting You. Right now, Lord, take the burden. We cast it upon You, knowing that You're better able to handle it than we ever will be. We ask that this time of prayer might make a difference in the balance of this day . . . which we commit to You now, in the name of Jesus, our Savior. Amen.

See also Psalm 40:1; Mark 1:35–39; 1 Timothy 2:1; 1 Peter 5:7; James 1:17; 5:13.

CRISIS INSPIRES PRAYER

It was in 1968 on an airplane bound for New York—normally a routine and really boring flight. As the plane was making its descent, the pilot realized the landing gear was not engaging. His plane was running low on fuel. He told the passengers to place their heads between their knees and grab their ankles just before impact.

Then, with the landing only minutes away, the pilot announced over the intercom: "We are beginning our final descent. At this moment, in accordance with International Aviation Codes established at Geneva, it is my obligation to inform you that if you believe in God you should commence prayer." That's *exactly* what he said!

I'm happy to report that the belly landing occurred without a hitch. No one was injured and, aside from some rather extensive damage to the plane, the airline hardly remembered the incident.

Amazing. The only thing that brought out into the open that "secret rule" was crisis. Pushed to the brink, back to the wall, right up to the wire, all escape routes closed . . . only then does our society crack open a hint of recognition that God may be there and—"if you believe . . . you should commence prayer."

There's nothing like crisis to expose the hidden truth of the soul. Any soul. We may mask it, ignore it, even pass it off with cool sophistication and intellectual denial . . . but take away the cushion of comfort, remove the shield of safety, interject the threat of death without the presence of people to take the panic out of the moment, and it's fairly certain that most in the ranks of humanity will "commence prayer."

57

Putting Down Pride

FOR ALL THAT IS IN THE WORLD, THE LUST OF THE FLESH AND
THE LUST OF THE EYES AND THE BOASTFUL PRIDE OF LIFE, IS NOT
FROM THE FATHER, BUT IS FROM THE WORLD. —1 JOHN 2:16

———————— ✺ ————————

OUR FATHER, THANK YOU *for using for Your glory those of
us who are given to ugly pride and controlling dominance. We also
thank You for finding ways to reduce our pride, either through Your
Word or through our experiences. I thank You that we can still be
who we are while we are engaged in exalting Christ and bringing
ourselves in line with Your desires for our lives.*

*As You rip from our hearts the self-satisfaction that we would
love to cling to, Father, and, as we bleed within, remind us that
nothing we surrender goes unrewarded. Remind us that as You
reduce us and crush us, You make us anew. You help us point our
lives to the Savior. Give us satisfaction in the roles You have placed us
in, and help us not to worry about being in some place of authority.*

Ultimately, exalt the name of Christ in our lives. At the same time, use Your Word and Your Spirit to humble us, enabling us to see our pride for what it is.

We praise You for Your work through Jesus. Amen.

See also Psalm 75:5; Proverbs 8:13; 29:23; 2 Corinthians 5:12.

SUCCESS BEGINS WITH HUMILITY

At the risk of sounding simplistic, I'd like to offer some counsel that stands diametrically opposed to today's "success" strategies. My suggestions will never appear in *BusinessWeek*, *Forbes*, or *Fortune*. Nevertheless, there's not a better formula for success known to man.

Here it is in twelve words: "God is opposed to the proud, but gives grace to the humble" (1 Peter 5:5). This verse is nestled in a context that addresses three realms related to true success (authority, attitude, anxiety).

First, regarding authority: *Submit yourself to those who are wise* (1 Peter 5:5). Listen to their counsel, be accountable and open to their reproofs, accept their suggestions, respect their seasoned years, and follow their model. Why? Because to strike out on your own, independent, self-determined journey can easily lead to pride, and "God is opposed to the proud."

Second, regarding attitude: *Humble yourself under God's mighty hand* (1 Peter 5:6). There is no more essential attitude for those wanting to be successful than this one. When we truly humble ourselves under God's mighty hand, wanting Him to grant us His kind of success in His own time and way, we refuse to manipulate circumstances or maneuver people by some hidden or deceptive scheme. We let God be God.

Third, regarding anxiety: *Throw yourself on the mercy and care of God* (1 Peter 5:7). Anxieties will come, count on it. Troubles, disappointments, and fears will emerge as you begin to be used by the Lord. So throw those anxieties back on the Lord! Cast your burdens on Him.

This scriptural game plan cuts cross-grain with today's promote-yourself propaganda. But when God is in charge, both the timing and the extent of whatever success He may have in mind for us will be surprising.

58

Putting First Things First

BUT SEEK FIRST HIS KINGDOM AND HIS RIGHTEOUSNESS, AND
ALL THESE THINGS WILL BE ADDED TO YOU. —MATTHEW 6:33

OUR FATHER, WE CONFESS *that placing Jesus first in our
lives precludes competition from all other loyalties: that no hobby or
occupation or pursuit—however engaging—can contain all of our
passion. No relationship—however intimate—can compete with
Christ for first place in our hearts. No possession—however prized—
can come between us and You.*

*Our Lord, we thank You for giving us our vocations—for the
privilege of making a living. We're grateful for the place where we
earn our wage and where we have the opportunity to live out our
faith. May our work become a platform upon which Your Son, Jesus
Christ, is placed on display day after day.*

And our relationships, Father, how vital they are—how valu-

able! We place them before You as well. May they be honoring to You.

May they represent associations that model the glory of Jesus Christ

rather than simply satisfy ourselves.

Regarding our ever-present battle with possessions—with

things: we place on the altar all the "stuff" of our lives. Help us in

forming our priorities, God. As we live in this physical world, help

us to put our possessions in their proper place, way down on the list of

what's important . . . after You—after all relationships.

And so, Lord, we lay before You our work, our relationships, and

our possessions. May they all be a part of the narrow path that leads

us to the way of the cross. We ask it in the name of Christ, our Lord.

Amen.

See also Deuteronomy 6:5; Haggai 1:3–9; Luke 8:14; 14:25–27; Philippians 3:8–13.

BEING BUSY

I have learned an ugly fact: busyness rapes relationships. It promises satisfying dreams but ends in hollow nightmares. It feeds the ego but starves the soul. It fills a calendar but fractures a family. It cultivates a program but destroys priorities.

My mentor, the late Dr. Howard Hendricks, once declared,

"Much of our activity these days is nothing more than a cheap anesthetic to deaden the pain of an empty life."

Searching words—but true. Want to change? Here's how:

First, *admit it*. You are too busy. Say it to yourself . . . your family . . . your friends. Openly and willingly *acknowledge* that it is wrong and something must be done—now.

Second, *stop it*. Starting today, refuse every possible activity that isn't absolutely necessary. Sound ruthless? So is the clock. So is your health. Start saying no. If feasible, resign from a committee or two . . . or three or four. Quit feeling so important. They'll get somebody else—or maybe they'll wise up and adopt a better plan.

Third, *maintain it*. It's easy to start fast and fade quickly. Watch over your time like a vulture. Discuss with your family some ways of investing hours with *them*—with the TV and smartphone and laptop off . . . without apologies for playing and laughing and doing nutty, fun things . . . without gobs of money having to be spent to "entertain" you.

Fourth, *share it*. You will soon discover some of the benefits of putting first things first. Tell others. Infect them with some germs of your excitement. Believe me, there are a lot of busy believers who would love to stop running if they only knew how.

Well, now we know. Let's be one of them.

59

Righteous Living

THEREFORE BE IMITATORS OF GOD, AS BELOVED CHILDREN;
AND WALK IN LOVE, JUST AS CHRIST ALSO LOVED YOU AND
GAVE HIMSELF UP FOR US, AN OFFERING AND A SACRIFICE
TO GOD AS A FRAGRANT AROMA. —EPHESIANS 5:1–2

OUR LORD AND MASTER, *we live in a world that's lost its way. We are impacted by it, we are influenced by it, and we are sometimes intimidated by it. So twisted is the thinking of society around us in this global atmosphere that it is easy to begin thinking we are the weird ones and the world is thinking straight. Help us each day to put that in proper order.*

Purify us, Father. In the process, guard us from foolish pride and from a superpious personality that comes across as fanatical, a personality disconnected from the real world. It's a tightrope we walk, Father. We need Your help to keep our balance, so that we don't turn off our neighbors with too much Scripture quoting or turn away a partner in life because of too much rigid preaching and not enough reasonable living. Help us know how to relate in the business world without compromising solid ethics and integrity. Make us people of our word in the details of life—like keeping our promises, like paying our bills, like respecting others, like cleaning up our foul language.

We need help, Lord, to overcome the bad habits of the past, to resist wanting to be liked rather than doing what's right, to be popular instead of being pure. And, Lord, in the process, may we continue to be easy to live with, winsome—like Christ, the most attractive individual who ever cast a shadow on earth. In great measure, Father, we trust You. For Jesus' sake, we pray. Amen.

See also Psalm 24:4–5; Proverbs 22:11; 1 Timothy 4:12; Titus 2:7.

PEER COURAGE

It's always easier to look at a dumb decision and call it such—after the fact. Once the smoke has cleared, anybody can see the issues. Hindsight is 20/20. Monday morning quarterbacks and armchair generals have the same two things in common: clear perspective and correct decisions. But given the same pressures, fears, insecurities, uncertainties, and group intimidation at the time everything is caving in, it's terribly hard to buck the tide while under the pressure from a group. Few are the Joshuas who will stand up and say, "As for me and my house . . ." (Joshua 24:15). Especially when nobody else is saying it. Or even thinking it.

Peer courage is the rare ability of a person to think and to act as a separate individual while under the influence of the surrounding group. Group pressure is a major motivation behind experimentation with drugs or sexual promiscuity or wholesale commitment to some cult or cooperation with an illegal financial scheme. It is terribly threatening. The screams and shouts of the majority have a way of intimidating the integrity of the few.

If it can happen among the upper crust of a nation, it should surprise no one that it can happen with ordinary folks like you and me. Be on guard! When push comes to shove, think independently. Better still, think biblically. We must do everything possible to lead with our head more than our feelings. If we fail to do this, we'll lose our ethical compass somewhere between our longing to be liked and our desire to do what is right.

It is not so hard to know what is right to do as to do what you know is right. If being a "team player" requires doing what's wrong, you're on the wrong team.

60

Overcoming Rebellion

HOW MANY ARE MY INIQUITIES AND SINS? MAKE KNOWN
TO ME MY REBELLION AND MY SIN. —JOB 13:23

LORD, YOU KNOW *that the human heart is rebellious. You are*
fully aware that this is a fallen world. We see evidence of it before our
very eyes on every evening news broadcast. We witness again and
again the ugly realities of stubbornness and resistance and selfishness.
We not only watch the flesh battle the flesh, but we're engaged in the
battle ourselves! Our Father, please give Your people the ability to
survive these difficult times.

Lord, help our fallen condition not cause us to compromise our
convictions in the delicate days of the future. May we stand on tiptoe,
like the ancient Hebrews, who heard the horn as it blew and saw
the smoke and the cloud and the lightning that flashed on Sinai and
realized that You are to be taken seriously. Find in us hearts will-

ing to do that. Give us unselfish generosity—greatheartedness—in the process of transitioning us from the way we were to the place we will be.

Lord, may we trust You completely. Just as Moses trusted You to get the Hebrews out of Egypt, so we trust You to get us into the promised land, bringing us safely to the other side of death, through bodily resurrection and on to new life in a new creation. Go before us, Lord, stay behind us, and surround us with what we need to overcome our rebellion. Give us a sense of peace and confidence that You are in the lead, not us. And cause us to trust You completely as we walk sensitively and humbly with You through the days before us. We ask it in Jesus' name. Amen.

See also Genesis 4:7; Exodus 19; Psalm 25:7; Ecclesiastes 8:12; Isaiah 1:5.

WHY WE WANDER

Depravity is not a sickness. It's death. Living death. It's death-like humanity—ugly, unashamed, uncovered, unrefined, unrepentant depravity. It's the blackness, the filthy cesspool of the unregenerate heart.

And let's not feel so smug. Just because you and I may not have murdered someone or pulled a multimillion-dollar bank job does not mean we don't have an evil nature.

You and I carry around killer natures within us. We, born spiritually dead and diseased by sin from our mother's womb, have the roots of wickedness deep down inside us. You do. I do. Every human does, including children (Psalm 51:5).

Given our own way, with no help from above and no restraints, we are capable of the most heinous acts imaginable. The same godless pollution that coursed through the minds of Hitler, Stalin, and Hussein, giving rise to despicable acts of prejudice and hatred, resides within us as well.

We've all got the same disease. Raw depravity is there in all its ugliness. Need a little biblical proof before you're willing to tolerate such an indictment? Stop and read Isaiah 64:6–7 and then Romans 3:9–18. When you do, you'll see yourself . . . in the raw. An untouched portrait within an inspired frame. If depravity were blue, we'd be blue all over.

Only after we read such a report can we appreciate the words we have become so familiar with. Maybe, with such a black backdrop, the gem will sparkle as never before.

Why would God possibly give His Son for such hopelessly lost sinners? How could He look past the hate and horror of our depravity?

The answer is one word. Grace.

61

The Lord Is Near

I CALLED ON YOUR NAME, O LORD, OUT OF THE LOWEST
PIT. YOU HAVE HEARD MY VOICE, "DO NOT HIDE YOUR
EAR FROM MY PRAYER FOR RELIEF, FROM MY CRY FOR
HELP." YOU DREW NEAR WHEN I CALLED ON YOU; YOU
SAID, "DO NOT FEAR!" —LAMENTATIONS 3:55–57

———————— ᴖ ————————

OUR FATHER, WE FIND RELIEF *in knowing that You're here.
We talk to You as though You are sitting right next to us. For indeed,
though we cannot see You, by faith we believe You're here. You bring
us such relief in life, our Father. We would be so lonely without You.
The nights would linger interminably; the pressure would be more
than we could bear. The tests would be incalculable were we on this
journey alone. But thankfully we're not.*

*You are here with us. And You are in control. We ask You to take
every part of that which makes us who we are . . . our temperaments,
our personalities, our gifts, our drives, our ambitions, our dreams, our*

failures, our hopes, our sorrows, our disappointments, and everything that makes up life for us. Take whatever we have, take whomever we love, take us wherever You find us, and let it all be set apart to You.

We ask You to take care of those people and situations that are beyond our ability to fix or change. Relieve our minds of the worry of it all, because, like thorns and briars that encroach upon a lovely garden and finally choke out its blooms, these things have a way of choking us so that we are unable to hear what You have to say.

We trust You to answer our prayer. In the merciful name of Jesus our Savior and our tender God, we pray. Amen.

See also Job 5:17–18; Psalm 94:12–14; 2 Thessalonians 1:6–8.

A MINISTRY OF ENCOURAGEMENT

His real name was Joseph. But everyone called him Barnabas—"son of encouragement." It's no wonder why. When the new, persecuted assembly at Jerusalem was backed to the wall and financially strapped, Barnabas sold a tract of land and donated the proceeds to the ministry (Acts 4:32–37). That's what we might call *encouragement in finances.*

Not afraid to stick his neck out for a new Christian who was suspect in the eyes of the majority, Barnabas brought Saul of Tarsus to Antioch and gave him a boost in leadership (Acts 11:22–26). This we might call *encouragement of fellowship*.

As Paul and Barnabas were about to begin another missionary journey, they discussed the possibility of taking along John Mark, the young man who earlier—to use Paul's words—"had deserted them" (Acts 13:13; 15:38). Paul refused. But Barnabas stood his ground, believing in this man's character, in spite of what happened before. They parted company over the issue, and Barnabas continued on with John Mark, modeling *encouragement in spite of failure*.

Oh, the need for encouragement today! Is there some soul you know in need of financial encouragement? A student? A young couple? A forgotten servant of God? Encourage generously!

What about someone who should be promoted to a place of greater usefulness but needs your endorsement? Go to bat for him! Give her a boost. Defend her character. She needs your fellowship.

Then there are the failures. Yes, they blew it. But are you big enough to extend a hand of encouragement and love? Lift up the failure with encouragement! It pays off! It did in John Mark's case. He later wrote the gospel of Mark and ultimately proved to be very useful—even to Paul (2 Timothy 4:11).

How essential is the ministry of encouragement!

62

God's Complete Control

GOD IS OUR REFUGE AND STRENGTH, A VERY PRESENT HELP
IN TROUBLE. THEREFORE WE WILL NOT FEAR, THOUGH THE
EARTH SHOULD CHANGE AND THOUGH THE MOUNTAINS
SLIP INTO THE HEART OF THE SEA; THOUGH ITS WATERS
ROAR AND FOAM, THOUGH THE MOUNTAINS QUAKE AT ITS
SWELLING PRIDE. . . . THE LORD OF HOSTS IS WITH US; THE
GOD OF JACOB IS OUR STRONGHOLD. —PSALM 46:1–3, 7

QUIET OUR HEARTS, DEAR FATHER, *and in so doing, remind
us that You are sovereign—not almost sovereign but altogether sovereign. Nothing occurs in our lives that has not been masterfully
planned and put together by You, our eternal God. Help us to enter
into the truth of Psalm 46:10 personally and consistently. May that
result in being still, enabling us to discover that You are God. As we
cast our cares upon You, knowing You care for us, release our stress.*

We entrust our concerns to You today . . . large and small, new and nagging. We long to experience peace-filled living by stepping off this treadmill called pressurized living. We pray that Your mighty presence would take the place of the stress, the demands, the struggles, the mess we've created. We ask that You would give us Your shalom—Your peace—like we've never known it before. We deliberately choose to trust You and to rest in You. In the name of Jesus, we pray. Amen.

See also Psalm 34:4; Proverbs 16:3; Jeremiah 17:7; Philippians 4:19.

———————— ⌁ ————————

HANDLING GRIEF CALMLY

Without announcement, adversity fell upon Job like an avalanche of jagged rocks. He lost his livestock, crops, land, servants, and—if you can believe it—all ten of his adult children. Soon thereafter he lost his health. Close your eyes for sixty seconds, and identify with that good man.

The book that bears his name records an incredible statement: "Through all this Job did not sin nor did he blame God" (1:22). How in the world could he handle such grief so calmly? At the risk of oversimplifying the situation, I suggest three basic answers.

First, *he claimed God's loving sovereignty.* He believed that the

Lord who gave had every right to take away (Job 1:21; 2:10). He looked up, claiming his Lord's right to rule over his life. To Job, God's sovereignty was interwoven with His love.

Second, *he counted on God's promise of resurrection* (Job 19:25–26). He looked ahead, counting on his Lord's promise to make all things bright and beautiful in the life beyond. He knew that at that time all pain, death, sorrow, tears, and adversity would be removed.

Third, *he confessed his own lack of understanding*. What a relief this brings! He didn't feel obligated to explain why. He looked within, confessing his inability to put it all together, not feeling forced to answer why.

Perhaps you are beginning to get nicked by falling rocks . . . maybe the avalanche has already fallen . . . maybe not. Adversity may seem a thousand miles away. That's the way Job felt a few minutes before it struck.

I urge you to review these thoughts as you turn out the lights tonight, my friend, just in case.

63

Fighting against Self-Focus

DO NOTHING FROM SELFISHNESS OR EMPTY CONCEIT, BUT
WITH HUMILITY OF MIND REGARD ONE ANOTHER AS MORE
IMPORTANT THAN YOURSELVES; DO NOT MERELY LOOK
OUT FOR YOUR OWN PERSONAL INTERESTS, BUT ALSO FOR
THE INTERESTS OF OTHERS. —PHILIPPIANS 2:3–4

OUR FATHER, WE WHO OPERATE *in such selfish realms often find ourselves preoccupied with stuff of our own. We focus on messes we've made back in the yesterdays of our lives, consumed with fears of tomorrow, knowing our propensity toward messing things up and uncertain about where this will lead. And then, of all things, in this ever-present now, we find ourselves again preoccupied with what someone may think . . . or say or do or how we will look in their eyes.*

Deliver us, Father, if only for today, from our preoccupation with self. Help us to envision You as King, the very essence of life—God who forgives all messes, who understands all frustrations, who calms all fears; King who reigns over our lives supremely. Because we have come to the cross and met You on Your terms, Lord, may we understand that Your will is really best, even when we cannot explain it, understand it, or for that matter, defend it. You're King. You're the Monarch, the Master. We are Your servants. You're the Potter; we're the clay.

Whatever we are dealing with today, quiet our spirits. Bring Your presence to our immediate attention. May it eclipse everything else. May Your sovereignty reassure us and Your hand on our life humble us.

In the great name of Your Son, Jesus, our King, our Lord, and our life, we pray. Amen.

See also Proverbs 23:6; Matthew 23:25; James 3:14, 16.

INTRUSIONS

If you question your selfishness, check your attitude toward intrusions. Those inevitable, unpredictable interruptions that make us irritable . . . especially when they persist, seizing our attention whether we are ready or not. And, if you're like me, usually we're not.

An intrusion is someone or something that thrusts itself into our world without permission, without an invitation, and it refuses to be ignored. Like an early morning knock at your door. Or a talkative passenger next to you on a long flight. Or an illness that strikes at the wrong time. But the most common intrusion? The relentless, constant demands of young children. Yes, constant. The child's need to be loved, to be answered, to be listened to, to be helped, held, corrected, trained, always encouraged, and occasionally disciplined.

I watched a young mother in a doctor's waiting room recently. She was pregnant and had a toddler plus one in diapers in her arms. She was one busy lady! Untied shoes, runny noses, twelve questions a minute, dropped rattle (five times), three falls (once on his face), loud crying, a juice bottle that spilled in the bag, and as she mopped it up with her last clean diaper, the baby barfed right down the back of her neck. With incredible patience, that mother hung in there. Her whole world was (and will continue to be) one gigantic intrusion.

Remember Jesus' words? "Whoever then humbles himself as this child, he is the greatest in the kingdom of heaven. And whoever receives one such child in My name receives Me" (Matthew 18:4–5). Yes, children are the finest illustrations Jesus could have used. He flatly declares that receiving them is tantamount to receiving Him. Obviously, He believes they are worth it all, no matter how many demands or how many intrusions.

64

A Heart of Service

EVEN THE SON OF MAN DID NOT COME TO BE SERVED, BUT TO

SERVE, AND TO GIVE HIS LIFE A RANSOM FOR MANY. —MARK 10:45

IT'S A PRETTY AWESOME THING, *Lord, to be in Your service.*
It's a lot easier to begin and run a company, even a big corporation,
than it is to serve the body of Christ. As humans, we see the outward
appearance, but You look at the heart. We reward achievements that
everybody notices, but You reward those things that nobody knows
about. You reward motives behind actions. You reward generosity that
is never publicly announced. You reward sacrifice, which is merely the
M. O. of a real servant. And so, Father, thank You for the joy of serv-
ing You—supporting Your work, believing in Your ministry, trusting
You with our whole hearts, and leaning not on our own understanding.

Guide us, O Lord. Our desire is to serve with quality, authen-
ticity, humility, grace, mercy, and compassion. May we serve better

in deeds than in words. Make us a people who have a heart for the whole world, not just our own little backyard. Guard us from acts of the flesh, from foolish decisions, from rash actions, from impatient reactions, from selfish motives. Lord, Your reputation is at stake, not ours. We hold You in highest esteem. Our desire is to know Christ intimately, and in knowing Him, to model His life of service in an authentic manner.

We pray this in His name. Amen.

See also Isaiah 32:17; Romans 12:1; Ephesians 2:8–10; 1 Timothy 1:12.

JUST BECAUSE YOU CARE

It was a cold night when Senator John Stennis, the hawkish Democrat, drove from Capitol Hill to his northwest Washington home. At precisely 7:40 p.m., Stennis parked his car and started walking toward his home fifty feet away.

Out of the darkness jumped two robbers. One nervously waved a .22-caliber pistol as the other relieved the senator of his wallet, a gold wristwatch, his Phi Beta Kappa key, and a quarter in change. Not only did they rob him, but they also shot him. Twice. The first slug tore through the senator's stomach. The second lodged in his left thigh. The assailants fled into the cold, black night as Stennis stumbled to his house.

The tragedy was reported over Republican Senator Mark Hatfield's car radio that wintry night. Disregarding the strong differences of conviction between himself and Senator Stennis, Hatfield raced to the hospital. He quickly scoped out the situation at the understaffed facility, spotted an unattended switchboard, sat down, and voluntarily went to work. He never gave anyone his name, because someone would surely suspect some ulterior political motive. He simply said it was his privilege to help someone he respected.

That story, though it happened years ago, offers a powerful model for us as Christians. Personal preferences and convictions may vary among members of the body, but we have a bond that binds us to one another. It is the glue of authentic love, expressing itself in compassion, willingness to support, and (when possible) coming to the aid of another. And what does it take? Being free of grudges, pettiness, vengeance, and prejudice. Seeing another in need—regardless of differences of opinion—and reaching out in solid Christian maturity. Just because you care.

65

Relief from Shame

"Let any one of you who is without sin be the first to throw a stone at her." Again he stooped down and wrote on the ground. At this, those who heard began to go away one at a time, the older ones first, until only Jesus was left, with the woman still standing there. Jesus straightened up and asked her, "Woman, where are they? Has no one condemned you?" "No one, sir," she said. "Then neither do I condemn you," Jesus declared. "Go now and leave your life of sin." —John 8:7–11 niv

---

We are grateful, Father, *that Your Son did not come to call the righteous but sinners to repentance. By Your grace, You have invited people who are imperfect, who are sinful, who have every reason to be ashamed of themselves, who are failures, who are guilty of wrong, to come to You and to find in You relief from their burdens, hope beyond the present, and relief from shame.*

Living in self-condemnation for something we have done wrong, we often forget, there is now no condemnation for those who are in Christ Jesus. So we pray, Father, that You will bring to Yourself those who have not yet found a way to silence the accusers within them— the thoughts that condemn as judge and jury. The tragedy is, when we hear those thoughts we believe them as true! Give us the first of several steps toward relief. May we find ultimately the joy of living by grace because of the finished work of Jesus Christ our Savior. In Jesus' name, we pray. Amen.

See also Zephaniah 3:19; Luke 5:32; Romans 8:1, 33–34.

GOD LOVES THE REAL US

A snowcapped mountain range may seem beautiful from a distance, but when you get close, you see a different scene entirely. Behind that beauty are screaming winds, bitter cold, blinding snow, huge boulders, icy roads, raw fear, and indescribable dangers. Distance feeds our fantasy. Any mountain range seems more beautiful when viewed from a sunlit street seventy-five miles away.

In the same way, we're all beautiful people from a distance. Well dressed, nice smile, friendly looking, cultured, under control, at peace. But what a different picture when someone comes close and gets in touch! What appeared placid is really a mixture of winding roads of insecurity and uncertainty, maddening gusts of lust, greed, self-indulgence, and pathways of pride often glazed over with a slick layer of hypocrisy—all shrouded in a cloud of fear of being found out. From a distance we dazzle . . . up close we're tarnished. Put enough of us together and we may resemble an impressive mountain range to the onlooker. But when you get down into the shadowy crevices . . . the Alps we ain't.

I'm convinced that's why our Lord means so much to us. He scrutinizes our path. He is intimately acquainted with all our ways. Darkness and light are alike to Him. Not one of us is hidden from His sight. All things are open and laid bare before Him: our darkest secret, our deepest shame, our stormy past, our worst thought, our hidden motive, our vilest imagination . . . even our vain attempts to cover the ugly with snow-white beauty. He comes up close. He sees it all. He knows our frame. He remembers we are dust. Amazingly, He loves us still.

66

Strength in the Battle against Evil

BE STRONG IN THE LORD AND IN THE STRENGTH OF HIS MIGHT. PUT ON THE FULL ARMOR OF GOD, SO THAT YOU WILL BE ABLE TO STAND FIRM AGAINST THE SCHEMES OF THE DEVIL. —EPHESIANS 6:10–11

ALMIGHTY GOD, *You are our all-powerful and invincible Lord. None can overcome You. None can stand against You. How we need You, especially when the battle against evil rages! Thank You for standing by our side, for being our strong shield and defender. We have no strength in ourselves. We face an adversary far more powerful, more brilliant, and more experienced than we. The enemy stands firmly against us, ready to attack at every weak point. We know that our enemy will not let up, that he will fight to the bitter end. And so, with confidence, we want to put on and wear the whole armor of God . . . and, in Your strength alone, we can resist the wicked forces that desire to bring us down.*

Give us new hope, Lord—hope that we can one day get beyond the struggle raging for our lives. We look forward to that day soon when Christ will once and for all win the victory that already belongs to Him because of the cross. Encourage us with the thought that, in Christ, we triumph! In His victorious name, we pray. Amen.

See also Luke 4:13; 2 Corinthians 4:16–18; Ephesians 4:26–27; 1 Peter 5:8–10.

ENDURANCE

Moses was one tough hombre. He refused to give in or give up. No amount of odds against him caused him to surrender.

That kind of resolve would be impressive if he were in his twenties or thirties, the time when "youths grow weary and tired, and vigorous young men stumble badly" (Isaiah 40:30). We would be even more impressed if Moses were in his forties or fifties—those "long, dull, monotonous years of middle-aged prosperity," which C. S. Lewis described as "excellent campaigning weather for the Devil."

But Moses *endured when he was in his eighties and beyond!* The old man was relentlessly resilient. He endured, despite the contempt of Pharaoh, the mightiest monarch of that era . . . despite the stubbornness of the hundreds of thousands of Hebrews who grumbled and rebelled . . . despite the criticism of those closest to him . . . despite the disappointments he personally encountered.

How did Moses do it? He fixed his heart and soul on the One who, alone, judges righteously. He continually reminded himself that his sole purpose in life was to please *Him* . . . to obey *Him* . . . to glorify *Him* . . . to gain *His* approval at all cost. Such lasting durability is rare but not impossible. Maybe the great apostle Paul had such things in mind when he introduced his classic essay on the armor of God by writing, "and having done everything . . . stand firm" (Ephesians 6:13).

Whatever it is you're facing, stand strong. Walk in quiet confidence, not veiled pride. Be certain without being stubborn . . . firm without becoming unteachable . . . enduring but not discourteous . . . full of truth balanced well with grace. Tough but also tender.

67

Compassion in Suffering

HE WAS DESPISED AND FORSAKEN OF MEN, A MAN OF SORROWS
AND ACQUAINTED WITH GRIEF; AND LIKE ONE FROM WHOM
MEN HIDE THEIR FACE HE WAS DESPISED, AND WE DID NOT
ESTEEM HIM. SURELY OUR GRIEFS HE HIMSELF BORE, AND
OUR SORROWS HE CARRIED; YET WE OURSELVES ESTEEMED HIM
STRICKEN, SMITTEN OF GOD, AND AFFLICTED. —ISAIAH 53:3–4

LORD, WORDS OF HOPE *from others can fall flat if things aren't
right in our own lives. When we're consumed by rage and resentment, somehow these words about joy and purpose sound hollow . . .
they seem meaningless. But when our hearts are right with You, we
have ears to hear the message of hope. Rather than resisting others'
words, we appreciate them, and we love You for sending them to us
in a time of need.*

*Father, truth be told, some of us are in great anguish. Give us
grace to match our trials—better still, to rise above them. Grant a*

sense of hope and purpose beyond our pain. Bless us with a fresh reminder that we are not alone . . . that Your plan has not been thwarted . . . that we have not been abandoned though our suffering gets worse, not better.

After You have strengthened us—and we are on our feet—help us maintain a compassion for those who suffer. Give us a listening ear and a word of encouragement for others living in this world of hurt. Remind us how we felt when we were there . . . and that Your plan may include for us another walk with You down the narrow and rugged path of suffering. And remind us that Your Son, though sinless, was acquainted with grief. We ask this in the compassionate name of the Man of Sorrows. Amen.

See also Proverbs 25:20; 2 Corinthians 1:3–7; Hebrews 12:3; 1 Peter 2:21.

COMPASSION BEFORE INFORMATION

It was one of those backhanded compliments. It came from a man who had listened to me speak during several sessions at a conference. Toward the end of the week, he and I had coffee together. It was then he risked telling me something straight. He blurted, "I don't get you, Swindoll. Even though you're a firm believer in the Bible, you're still having fun. You've even got some compassion."

That last statement really got me thinking. He referred to "compassion" as though it wasn't supposed to be there. Like, if you're committed to the truth of Scripture, you shouldn't concern yourself with the needs of people. Don't sweat all the people stuff—discouragement, heartaches, illness, and grief—because those are only temporal problems. Our job is to give 'em the gospel. Don't get sidetracked by their pain and problems, just keep preaching the truth!

Be honest now. Isn't that the way it usually is? Isn't it a fact that the more conservative one becomes, the less compassionate?

I want to know when we departed from the biblical model. When did we begin to ignore Christ's care for the needy? When did we opt for placing more emphasis on proclamation and less on compassion?

To quote a familiar axiom: others won't care how much we know until they know how much we care. Let's put compassion right up there alongside information. We need both, but in the right order. Let's allow compassion to create a hunger for the truth. We'll be in good company. That's exactly what Jesus did with you and me and a bunch of other sinners who deserved and expected condemnation but got compassion instead.

68

Victory over Temptation

No temptation has overtaken you but such as is common to man; and God is faithful, who will not allow you to be tempted beyond what you are able, but with the temptation will provide the way of escape also, so that you will be able to endure it. —1 Corinthians 10:13

———————— ⟳ ————————

Thank You, Father, *for Your penetrating truth preserved through the centuries. Thank You for the careful concern of a man like the apostle Peter who knew both sides of life on planet Earth: what it was like to live in this old world and what it was like to walk with the Savior, Your Son. Thank You for Peter's admonishment to prepare our minds for action, keep sober in spirit, fix our hope on Your grace, and not to conform our lives to the former lusts . . . but to be holy as You are. Thank You for Paul's confidence that You won't allow temptation to push us into an inescapable corner.*

Lord, because You don't save us and then suddenly take us home to heaven but leave us here on earth, hear us as we ask You to bring to our attention those things that will assist us in staying clean in a corrupt world. Give us an intense distaste for things that displease You. At the same time give us a renewed pleasure in things that uphold Your honor and magnify Your truth. As You do this, we will have what we crave: victory over temptation. We ask this in the name of Him who consistently and victoriously withstood the relentless blast of the devil's temptations, Jesus our Lord. Amen.

See also Matthew 4:1–11; 1 Peter 1:13–16; 5:8–9; 2 Peter 2:9.

CURIOSITY

Curiosity is the sign of a healthy, ingenious mind. It's the built-in teacher that instantly challenges the status quo . . . that turns a wayward waif into a Winston Churchill, a hopeless mute into a Helen Keller, and a Missouri farm boy into a Walt Disney. Curiosity is essential to progress.

And yet . . . what a deceitful role curiosity can play! Remove the safety belt of biblical restraint and curiosity sends our vehicle of learning on a collision course for disaster. It has a way of making us meddle in others' affairs. It dresses wrong in the most attractive apparel known to man. It hides the damnable consequences of adultery behind the alluring garb of pleasure and companionship. It masquerades the heartaches of alcoholism by dressing them in the context of relaxation and social fun. Curiosity is the most-needed commodity depended upon to keep the world of the occult busy and effective.

Curiosity is as much a part of human nature as the elbow is a part of the arm. Our enemy knows that and counts on it. He knows how much we believe the old line: "I need to satisfy my curiosity." He's a master at the black art of subterfuge, a two-bit word for setting a trap that makes our curiosity sit up and get sucked in. Remember, he's been setting traps a lot longer than you and I have been dodging them. If he can garnish the hook with the right bait—designed to arouse just enough of our curiosity—*it's only a matter of time.*

Of course, we need not be the stupid victims of our foolish curiosity . . . but we will never read that warning written on the trap signed by the surgeon general of Beelzebub. Satan's a genius trap setter. Let's take God at His Word: when it comes to sin, our curiosity doesn't need to be satisfied.

69

Protection and Strength in the Face of Terrorism

"CEASE STRIVING AND KNOW THAT I AM GOD; I WILL
BE EXALTED AMONG THE NATIONS, I WILL BE EXALTED IN
THE EARTH." THE LORD OF HOSTS IS WITH US; THE GOD
OF JACOB IS OUR STRONGHOLD. —PSALM 46:10–11

———————— ༄ ————————

OUR GOD, AS NEVER BEFORE *in this generation, we are
dependent upon You for protection and strength. Though the mountains quake, though bridges fall, though tunnels are destroyed, though
ships sink, though there will be the loss of life, though there will be the
threat of war invading, though there are even at this time terrorists
and enemies within our midst, we will not fear. Our resolve is firm
because our refuge lies in the eternal foundation of the living God.*

*We pray for parents. Strong and brave, may they stand. May
they set their hearts on You for the protection of their offspring, especially those who serve in the military. We pray for loved ones and*

family members and friends who grieve the loss of those taken in ter-
rorist acts and in fierce combat on the battlefield.

We pray that You will give our national leaders and their advi-
sors great courage and wisdom. Give us sufficient trust and confi-
dence to follow them. May our country and our world remain united
as evil is assaulted and as we fall on our knees in humble repentance
before You. In the process of giving us victory, we pray that You will
purge our nation. Bring us before You in humble trust and remind us
over and over again that God is our refuge and strength, a very pres-
ent help in trouble. We ask this confidently in the name of Christ, our
Victorious Warrior. Amen.

See also Psalm 46:1; 121:1–8; Matthew 10:28; Romans 8:35–39; 1 Timothy 2:1–4.

TRUE SECURITY

Every year when September 11 shows up on my calendar, I remember Psalm 11. As David wrote this psalm, King Saul was probably hunting him.

Hiding somewhere in the Judean wilderness, David penned the words: "If the foundations are destroyed, what can the righteous do?" (Psalm 11:3). Great question! Destroy the building's foundations, and you topple the building. But David wasn't referring to structures; he was writing this psalm about life. David meant this: if the foundation of a life is destroyed, that life crumbles. But if the foundation remains secure, no amount of stress—in David's case, no attack by Saul—can cause a life to fracture and fall. Psalm 11 reveals that David could feel this truth being put to the test. But he wasn't brought down . . . because the foundations of his life were strong.

If those foundations hadn't been secure, his life would've collapsed, dropped like a sack of sand. How do I know his foundations were secure? Look at the first verse: "In the LORD I take refuge" (11:1). A refuge is a place of hiding, a place of protection. The ancient Hebrew term—*chasah*—means a protective place that provides safety from whatever would hit and hurt. It's a protective shield from danger and distress. David made it clear that his Lord was his *chasah*. Because that was true, David knew his foundations were sure.

We can know the same. No matter how insecure and chaotic our times may be! No matter if terrorists topple our buildings or kill our fellow citizens! No matter if God doesn't fully answer our question, *why*. On the solid foundation of our sovereign God—and *only* there—we are safe and secure.

70

The Value of God's Word

Your word I have treasured in my heart, that I may not sin against You. . . . I will meditate on Your precepts and regard Your ways. I shall delight in Your statutes; I shall not forget Your word. —Psalm 119:11, 15–16

꘏

How precious is Your Word *to us, our Father. The older we get, the more we realize its value and treasure its truths. We thank You for Your precepts, clearly delineated and purposefully defined in Scripture to give us direction. Thank You also for principles that, with wisdom, may be applied even in the twenty-first century, when it seems as though the world's standard for living has gotten fuzzy, making the future intimidating and frightening for many.*

We're grateful, Lord, that Your Word gives light, because there's an enormous amount of darkness around us. We want to live on the bright side of life. We want to enjoy what You have for us rather than endure our circumstances. We want to see the beauty of Your pur-

poses and how they all fit together into a divinely designed plan that makes great sense to You. We rest our case there, even though there are times it does not make sense to us.

Thank You, Father, for the way You speak to us through Scripture. May we realize its relevance and appreciate how often Your Word addresses the needs of our lives. In clearly stated words, it talks about where we live, how we are to live, and what life is all about. We desperately need that guidance. So we submit ourselves to You and we commit ourselves to the reading and the study of Your Word. May we be faithful and disciplined to this commitment.

In the name of Jesus, we pray. Amen.

See also Luke 24:27; John 5:39; 2 Timothy 3:16; 1 Peter 2:2.

DISCOVERING PRICELESS WISDOM

Howard Carter's mouth and eyes opened wide as he heard his aide's question.

For more than a score of centuries, archaeologists, tourists, and tomb robbers had searched for the burial places of Egypt's pharaohs. It was believed that nothing remained undisturbed. But somehow he was convinced there was one remaining tomb. And then, finally . . . *Eureka!*

Peering into the silent darkness, Howard Carter saw what no modern human had ever seen. Standing a few feet behind him, his aide asked, "Can you see anything?" What a question! Wooden animals, statues, chests, gilded chariots, carved cobras, vases, daggers, jewels, a throne . . . even a hand-carved coffin depicting on its golden lid a teenage king. Everywhere was the glint of gold. It was, of course, the world's most exciting archaeological discovery: the tomb and treasure of King Tutankhamen.

There are few joys like the joy of sudden discovery. Instantly forgotten is the pain and expense of the search, the inconveniences, the long hours, the many sacrifices. Lost in the thrill of the moment, we relish the inexpressible finding like a little child watching a spider.

Solomon wrote about the greatest discovery of all: the treasure of Scripture. "My son, if you will receive my words . . . If you seek [wisdom] as silver and search for her as for hidden treasures; then you will discern the fear of the LORD and discover the knowledge of God" (Proverbs 2:1, 4–5).

Talk about a discovery! Hidden in Scripture are vaults of priceless wisdom that won't be found if you're in a hurry. But godly truth is there, awaiting discovery. God's Word, like a deep, deep mine, remains ready to yield its treasures.

Can you see anything?

71

Leaving a Legacy of Trust

HOW BLESSED IS THE MAN WHO HAS MADE THE LORD
HIS TRUST, AND HAS NOT TURNED TO THE PROUD, NOR TO
THOSE WHO LAPSE INTO FALSEHOOD. —PSALM 40:4

———————— ༒ ————————

OUR HEAVENLY FATHER, HOW GRATEFUL *we are for Your*
Son, Jesus. Where would we be without Him? How could we oper-
ate our lives without firm confidence in Him? It is sweet to trust in
Jesus, to take Him at His word. And we willingly do that, Father.
We release to You the pressures of the home and the office, the unex-
plained events, the mysteries that remain unsolved. We still trust
You. For answers that we have not yet experienced, we trust You. To
bring about the desires of our hearts which we are unable to do for
ourselves, we trust You, Father.

We take You at Your word. What You have promised, You will
fulfill. What You have written, You will keep. And You have made
Your Word known to us in our own tongue so that we can read it, not

simply in black print on white pages but as truth to live by and, if necessary, to die for.

May our children remember us as parents who loved You—as parents who brought them up in a way that pleased You. Help our children to grow and learn to respect You, to have a deep and abiding trust in You, just as we have. How easily the church can become a greenhouse where growth seems normal and predictable, yet it is far removed from the real world. Help us to bridge for our children what it means to live for Christ in a world that has long since lost its way.

It is sweet to trust in Jesus, and we do so, Father, with all our hearts. In His great name, we pray. Amen.

See also Psalm 37:5; 56:3; Proverbs 3:5–6; Isaiah 12:2.

———————— ·ֵ· ————————

WHO'S IN CHARGE HERE?

It's easy to get confused these days. "Out of control" isn't what we want to be. People who drink too much are said to be "out of control." The same goes for those who take things to an extreme: prescription drugs, food, fitness, sex, spending, work—you name it.

But wait. Does this mean we're supposed to be "in control"? Is that our goal? Before you answer, consider. I know a number of bosses who are definitely "in control." Folks who work for them either decide to grin and bear it or they jump ship as soon as another job surfaces. Some fathers are, without question, "in control." They intimidate, dominate, and manipulate. Mothers-in-law are notoriously known for this—not all, but many. They are usually the same ones who control their husbands.

A healthy, happy life requires being in control of ourselves . . . but not controlling of others. Our example? Christ, of course. He got the job done. Without wasted effort, personal panic, or extreme demands, He stayed in control of His objective. Right on schedule, He went to that cross. But the vast majority of people back then, as now, didn't give Christ the time of day. Could He have grabbed the controls and forced them to sit up and take notice? Absolutely. But it was His perfect control that restrained Him from controlling others.

In brief, the Christian life boils down to a battle of the wills: Christ's versus our own. Every day we live we must answer, "Who's in charge here?" To say that He is means we leave the driving to Him . . . which includes the vehicle, the map, the route, the destination, the whole journey. That's trust.

Be honest now. Have you surrendered control to Him today?

72

Standing Alone for the Truth

SHADRACH, MESHACH AND ABED-NEGO REPLIED TO THE KING,
"O NEBUCHADNEZZAR, WE DO NOT NEED TO GIVE YOU AN ANSWER
CONCERNING THIS MATTER. IF IT BE SO, OUR GOD WHOM WE
SERVE IS ABLE TO DELIVER US FROM THE FURNACE OF BLAZING
FIRE; AND HE WILL DELIVER US OUT OF YOUR HAND, O KING.
BUT EVEN IF HE DOES NOT, LET IT BE KNOWN TO YOU, O KING,
THAT WE ARE NOT GOING TO SERVE YOUR GODS OR WORSHIP THE
GOLDEN IMAGE THAT YOU HAVE SET UP." —DANIEL 3:16–18

———————— ꙮ ————————

OUR FATHER IN HEAVEN, *as a result of Your Word we pray*
that You might grant to us insight into our homes, our nation, and
this world. We ask You to raise up from this world that is given to
passivity and compromise a body of people who will live for and, if
necessary, fight for the truth. I pray that we might not embrace the
false philosophies of our day, which sound so logical and appealing

but in the end turn us into passive fools. We pray, our Father, that we might become balanced believers, discerning times in which it is necessary to be very still and quiet; times in which it is essential to say, "Lord, this is Your battle. Please take this for me"; and other times when the issue is such that we say, "Even if I must stand alone, I will stand. Even if it means I will be beaten to the death, I will take that, because an issue greater than all is at stake."

Thank You for the reminder of women and men in uniform who fight courageously so that we might enjoy the freedom of worship. Father, steel us. Put strength and integrity where there has been weakness. Replace the flab and the fat of our day with the muscle of conviction. And, Lord, may You raise up from our homes young people who have convictions that reach deeper than any persuasive word of the world. Through Christ, we pray. Amen.

See also Ecclesiastes 3:3, 8; 1 Corinthians 1:20–21; 3:19; James 4:17; 2 Timothy 2:3–4.

DECISIVENESS

There will always be some who want others to make their decisions for them. Many Christians are continually looking for some evangelical guru or superstar pastor to cosign for their lives.

For a leader, it takes the restraining power of the Holy Spirit to withstand such tempting invitations to take control. It is helpful to remember that every time we yield to the temptation of power, we hinder others' growth toward maturity. Making one's own decisions develops healthy mental and spiritual muscles. But, I repeat, there will always be a few who crave to be told what to do. They remain so indecisive their favorite color is plaid.

A major reason some prefer to be indecisive is laziness. Decision making is hard work, requiring a painful, exacting process rare to many, called *thinking*. How much easier it is to adopt a list, to click off the answers—one, two, three, four, five. All you need to do is follow instructions. Don't weigh the consequences. Just do as you are told. Don't think it through and decide . . . just submit. Bad plan.

Decisiveness is far too often replaced with blind obedience, unquestioned authority, and absolute loyalty. There is a place for that philosophy in the military where there isn't time to stop and think. Rap sessions aren't too popular in combat when the objective is survival. But in day-to-day living, when issues are not clearly spelled out in Scripture, when there is a lot of gray instead of black and white, we need to learn how to be decisive.

I urge you to think wisely. Understand the risks. Weigh the alternatives. Choose for yourself. *You* decide.

73

Unity among God's People

THERE IS ONE BODY AND ONE SPIRIT, JUST AS ALSO YOU WERE
CALLED IN ONE HOPE OF YOUR CALLING; ONE LORD, ONE FAITH,
ONE BAPTISM, ONE GOD AND FATHER OF ALL WHO IS OVER
ALL AND THROUGH ALL AND IN ALL. —EPHESIANS 4:4–6

OUR FATHER, WHAT A GREAT PRIVILEGE *we have been
provided by Your amazing grace, that You are making us one together
with such a wide and diverse group of people! Thank You for the mystery now being made known to Your people, how You have drawn
together Jew and Gentile all into one body, to be unified in the family
over which Christ is Master and Head. We find great comfort in that
because as our Master, Jesus will safeguard us, will care for us, will
treat us honorably. Thank You for Your tender mercies, Your compassions that are new every morning.*

*We find great joy, Lord, in being a body of Your people brought
together for transformation and service. We come with various colors*

and backgrounds and struggles and sins. We stand on a level plane at the foot of the cross. May our unity with other believers be so palpable, our fellowship so genuine, and our hearts so winsome and warm that people without Christ are irresistibly drawn to Your Son, whom we love and adore. In His name, we pray. Amen.

See also Psalm 133:1; John 17:23; Ephesians 3:3–6; Colossians 3:14.

WHAT'S THE BIG DEAL?

Haven't you wondered at times if the church is *that* big a deal? I sure have. I mean, compared to the keen-thinking scientific, educational, and political minds that impact humanity, of what importance are a few dozen people in some white, clapboard building singing "In the Sweet By and By"?

Yet, unless we've recently excised Matthew 16:18 from our Bibles, it still says what Jesus said. It includes a promise that the church is His personal project and that it will be perpetually invincible. That means all these other hot items, no matter how impressive and intimidating, will ultimately cool off and be replaced.

Years ago I heard my longtime friend Jay Kesler give a splendid talk entitled "Why I Believe in the Local Church." I pass along his five reasons to you. First, where else will you hear truth about death, judgment, relationships, meaning in life, and eternal destinies? Second, the church gives dignity to mankind in a day when humanity is lost in a meaningless quest for self. Third, it provides a moral compass in a society awash in relativism. Fourth, in the church people unselfishly care, because the Spirit of God is at work, weaving lives together. Fifth, more than any other institution, the church has provided schools, hospitals, and organizations of mercy.

No, the church isn't perfect (we're part of it, aren't we?) and it hasn't always modeled its message. But whatever is next in order of importance is a distant second—and I mean way down the line.

See you Sunday. That's when the body and the Head meet to celebrate this mysterious union when ordinary, garden-variety folks like us gather around the preeminent One. No matter how it may appear to others, if it's something God has chosen, it *is* a big deal.

74

Acknowledging Our Weakness

INDEED HE WAS CRUCIFIED BECAUSE OF WEAKNESS, YET HE LIVES BECAUSE OF THE POWER OF GOD. FOR WE ALSO ARE WEAK IN HIM, YET WE WILL LIVE WITH HIM BECAUSE OF THE POWER OF GOD DIRECTED TOWARD YOU. —2 CORINTHIANS 13:4

OUR FATHER, WE ALL STRUGGLE *with weakness. We're reminded almost every day that we don't have it all together. We need You. We have heartaches and disappointments that haven't gone away . . . the grief of broken relationships, illnesses, and recent deaths. We invite You to enter in, Lord. Enter into all of that on our behalf. Through Your presence may we find relief and release from that which has bound us, tied us up within. We're able to take only so much, and sometimes we come to a virtual breaking point. In our times of physical and emotional weakness, we need Your comfort and Your strength.*

We are also stalked by sin. We need Your grace. Sin has taken a terrible toll on the human condition. And though we are well-versed in every possible way of ignoring it or explaining it away, today we come to terms with it. Surely we have failed or fallen in some area just this week, and the ache of that nags us and troubles us—some needless words, some outburst of anger, some lingering resentment, or some caustic response.

Lord, thank You for the blood of Christ that keeps on cleansing us from all sins, including these. Forgive us, our Father. Remove from us the enemy's desire to make us ashamed and to drag us under the load of that failure. May we remember that in Your grace You not only forgive, but You wipe the slate clean. Thank You that You know our weakness and love us nevertheless. In the name of Jesus, we pray. Amen.

See also Romans 8:26; 15:1; 1 Corinthians 1:25; Hebrews 4:15.

PRESSING ON IN WEAKNESS

I recall a time, way back in 1980, when Cynthia was told she needed a breast biopsy. Since her mother died of breast cancer, we have always entertained a sensitivity about that similar fate striking my wife. Well, *I hit bottom!* Fear's ugly head arose and dealt a damnable blow to my otherwise peaceful spirit. I called a quick pastoral staff meeting and tried the old stiff-upper-lip approach as I told them what we were facing. My communication failed miserably. Instead of describing what was before us in a deliberate and objective manner, I broke into tears. The best I could do was mumble something about the procedure, admit my fears, and choke out a closing comment, "I'm sorry . . . I just can't seem to get a handle on this." I stood up and quietly walked out, embarrassed at my weakness of leadership.

To my surprise, one of the men followed me out the door. He was weeping as he said, "Chuck, you don't always have to *have a handle* on everything." He embraced me with genuine understanding. It was an important lesson to me. (By the way, that lump was *benign*.)

Even today, it seems like a guy my age could "get hold of himself" and remain professionally objective. I mean, after more than fifty years in the ministry, you would think I would have seen enough to toughen up. After so many bloody skirmishes and sleepless nights enduring the enemy's surprise attacks, even the greenhorn marine gets battle hardened. I must be getting soft. I still haven't discovered the secret of staying emotionally objective. I still cry.

We must face these perilous times head on. Even in our weaknesses, we must do whatever is necessary to stand firm, regardless. But there is no sin in shedding tears.

75

The Blessing of Abiding Hope

THE GRACE OF GOD HAS APPEARED, BRINGING SALVATION
TO ALL MEN, INSTRUCTING US TO DENY UNGODLINESS AND
WORLDLY DESIRES AND TO LIVE SENSIBLY, RIGHTEOUSLY AND
GODLY IN THE PRESENT AGE, LOOKING FOR THE BLESSED
HOPE AND THE APPEARING OF THE GLORY OF OUR GREAT
GOD AND SAVIOR, CHRIST JESUS. —TITUS 2:11–13

———————— ༄ ————————

FATHER, SHOW US AGAIN *the hope that is in the Savior. Calm the minds of those who are anxious, lest they fear that which they have no reason to fear. But for those who live in a false kind of security and with a smug sophistication, for those who think,* Someday I'll deal with this, *may misery dog their steps. Offer them no relief and no peace, as You, Spirit of God, bring them to their knees . . . so they might be brought to faith. Direct their hope to the only true source of hope in this world: Jesus Christ.*

Thank You for the hope that Your people have because of the Savior. May it not make us indifferent and distant from the lost; on the contrary, may we be sensitive, available, in touch, aware, in step with today. Keep us clearheaded, compassionate, and willing to help. Allow Your hope to penetrate to the deepest recesses of our souls. And as the knowledge of the soon return of Jesus grows within us, prompt us to be people who live out that hope—for ourselves, for others, and for You. We're grateful for truth and how it delivers us from error and needless fear. May we not become indifferent to the desperation of those around us, as we become acutely aware of the many needs throughout our world. In the compassionate name of Jesus, we pray. Amen.

See also Psalm 31:24; 42:5; Proverbs 24:14; Romans 5:4–5.

A RESURRECTION DAY HOPE

Easter never arrives without its refreshing reminder that there is a life beyond this one. True life. Eternal life. Glorious life. Those who live on what we might call the "outskirts of hope" need a transfusion—a hope transfusion. Easter gives it.

There are those who grieve over the recent loss of a loved one. Death has come like a thief, snatching away a treasured presence and leaving only hollow memories. What is missing? Hope. There is nothing like Easter to bring it back to life.

I cannot explain what happens, nor do I need to try. The simple fact is this: there is something magnificent, therapeutic, and reassuring about Easter morning. When Christians gather in houses of worship and lift their voices in praise to the risen Redeemer, declaring, "He is risen!" the demonic hosts of hell and their prince of darkness are temporarily paralyzed. When pastors stand and declare the unshakable, undeniable facts of Jesus' bodily, miraculous resurrection and the assurance of ours as well, the empty message of skeptics and cynics is momentarily silenced. An almost mysterious surge of power floods over us. The benefits are innumerable. To list a few:

- Our fears fade and release their grip.

- Our grief over those who have gone on is diminished.

- Our desire to press on in spite of the obstacles is rejuvenated.

- Our differences of opinion are eclipsed by our similar faith.

- Our identity as Christians is strengthened as we stand in the lengthening shadows of saints down through the centuries, who answer back in antiphonal voice: *"He is risen, indeed!"*

On Easter, a powerful hope transfusion awaits us. It happens every year. *Alleluia!*

76

Overcoming Hypocrisy

BE ESPECIALLY CAREFUL WHEN YOU ARE TRYING TO BE
GOOD SO THAT YOU DON'T MAKE A PERFORMANCE OUT OF
IT. IT MIGHT BE GOOD THEATER, BUT THE GOD WHO MADE
YOU WON'T BE APPLAUDING. —MATTHEW 6:1 MSG

LORD GOD, WE THANK YOU *for the model of Jesus Christ our
Savior, who, when He walked this earth, was draped with authenticity. We long to be authentic as our Savior was—not phony and
proud and faking our commitment to You but with a faith that's
genuine, not counterfeit. That takes courage. It takes guts to live the
real life before a world that's lost its way, where hypocrisy is so often
modeled and comes across as religious piety.*

*Forgive us, Father, for the way we have subtly sought the
applause of others, hoping they'd be impressed with our humility or
our generosity or even our authenticity, which wasn't that at all. We
pray that we'll be more effective in secret than we ever could be in*

public and that as a result of Your seeing us in secret, You'll be honored and the rewards will come at a time when it's just between You and us.

·Father, we pray that You will turn reproof into restoration and thereby change us so that we become like Christ—and unlike the Pharisees who were so impressed with themselves. May we instead be so impressed with You that we lose sight of ourselves. And in that self-forgetful state, may we give You all the glory You deserve. It is in the strong name of Jesus Christ that we pray. Amen.

See also Matthew 6:4–18; 23:13–51; Romans 12:9; James 3:17; 1 Peter 2:1–2.

THE DARK SIDE

Mark Twain used a word picture I've never forgotten: "Everyone is a moon, and has a dark side which he never shows to anybody." For the hypocrite, for those to whom cover-up is all-important, this dark side exists for years behind carefully guarded masks. Only a few know the facts . . . sometimes no one. But once the truth is exposed in all its ugliness, the shock factor is huge. Those who had been devotees become disillusioned over the hypocrisy.

Death exposed the other side of Elvis Presley's moon, bringing to light what had been hidden for years. *Life* magazine's feature article in June 1990 was yet another reminder of how much difference there can be between polished image and frightening reality. Appropriately titled "Down at the End of Lonely Street," the account documented how the man existed in a nightmarish cave of depression and despair, which massive doses and injections of drugs made bearable.

Because neither you nor I are invulnerable to hypocrisy's lure, allow me to drive this home. The lesson in all this is obvious: the safest route to follow is Authenticity Avenue, walled on either side by Sincerity and Vulnerability. The alternate route dead-ends at Lonely Street, the bleak scenery of which is best stated in a seldom-mentioned verse from the ancient book of Numbers: "Be sure your sin will find you out" (32:23). Haunting thought, but oh, so true.

I cannot explain how or why, I only know that rattling skeletons don't stay in closets . . . and lies don't remain private . . . and affairs don't stay secret . . . and hidden acts of darkness finally come to light. When they do, the stomachs of hypocrites start to churn, knowing it's only a matter of time before the whole truth, in all its ugliness, is exposed.

77

Personal Integrity

FROM THE CARE OF THE EWES WITH SUCKLING LAMBS
HE BROUGHT [DAVID] TO SHEPHERD JACOB HIS PEOPLE,
AND ISRAEL HIS INHERITANCE. SO HE SHEPHERDED THEM
ACCORDING TO THE INTEGRITY OF HIS HEART, AND GUIDED
THEM WITH HIS SKILLFUL HANDS. —PSALM 78:71–72

FATHER, PERSONAL PURITY *is never automatic or easily produced. Integrity doesn't flow from our flesh naturally or freely. In fact, many of us have lived too many days of our lives in hypocrisy and deception. That's why we need You so desperately. We don't know how to unravel the mess of our bad habits or untie the knots of our past, so we're tempted to continue ignoring Your convicting voice and living lives of regret. But enough is enough! We are determined to ignore it no longer. We refuse to wade any longer in shallow pools of carnality. Beginning today we are determined to live a life of integrity. We ask You to honor our decision to walk with You, to cease our life of duplicity, to stop compromising our integrity. Give us Your*

strength, dear Father, Your help, Your courage, Your wisdom. Forgive

our foolish and hypocritical ways. Deliver us from the dangerous and

deep quicksand of deceitful sin and establish us on the solid rock of

vulnerability and integrity.

May Your grace keep us from a judgmental spirit toward others,

Lord. Give us the encouragement we need to be all You have called

us to be as Your obedient children, so that we, like David with the

sheep, might guide others skillfully and well. In the strong name of

Jesus Christ our Lord, we pray. Amen.

See also Job 8:20; Psalm 15:1–2; Proverbs 2:6–7; 10:9; 20:7.

MORAL EXCELLENCE

Occasionally, I have had the honor to minister to high-ranking military officials serving in the Pentagon. These leaders are models of strong Christian commitment. During one discussion, the subject of moral purity surfaced. I asked if, in their ranks, a failure in character qualities was all that significant. "Of course!" they immediately responded. Their commitment to personal integrity impressed me because it was expressed spontaneously and sincerely. I told them they would make great pastors.

Suddenly the group became awkwardly quiet. One of the men finally broke the silence. He said the conversation touched a nerve since most of the officers in our group attended the same church— "one with a history of biblical preaching, wonderful fellowship, and a healthy testimony in the community, *until* ..." My stomach churned. I didn't want to guess what he would say next. He continued, "... until our pastor had an affair, and he and the woman both walked away from their mates and children." Tears, embarrassed looks, and slowly shaking heads revealed their bewilderment and deep disappointment. Their burden weighed heavily upon me. I felt embarrassed.

I was humiliated to think that a standard of high moral character is of paramount importance among military officers, but within the ranks of the clergy—my colleagues—an impurity epidemic rages.

This isn't the time to mince words. We all need the reminder of Paul's admonition: "For this is the will of God ... that you abstain from sexual immorality" (1 Thessalonians 4:3). Let's also remember Peter's urgent plea: "in your faith supply moral excellence" (2 Peter 1:5). Pay attention to being faithful, no matter where you serve. Whether in the military, the ministry, the marketplace, or the home—be faithful.

78

Remembering the Fallen

GREATER LOVE HAS NO ONE THAN THIS, THAT ONE LAY
DOWN HIS LIFE FOR HIS FRIENDS. —JOHN 15:13

———————— ᭦ ————————

TO THE END OF OUR LIVES, *our Father, we will be grateful for those who have taken liberty seriously. They stepped away from home and family—away from the love of a mom and dad, or of a spouse and children—and stepped into battle to defend freedom by giving their lives.*

We honor You, our Father, for giving us those of whom this world was not worthy. May each Memorial Day be more than just a celebration of eating and relaxing with family and friends. May we come aside on such occasions, pause, and reflect.

We recognize that there is much evil in this world, but we thank You that this planet is still under Your control. Thank You, dear Lord, for Your presence and Your sovereign hand, whether we are at war or in a time of peace. Help us to endure these difficult times in which we live with determination and faithfulness.

In addition to those who have fallen, we ask that You protect those who carry on the fight, those whose presence would eclipse any of ours. They are in hard places today and we thank You for each brave warrior. Thank You for our country that is still free, living in the legacy of such heroism.

We dedicate our lives to You and we do so with gratitude, because You have been so faithful to us. In the name of Jesus, we pray. Amen.

See also 2 Samuel 1:25–27; John 15:13; 2 Timothy 2:4.

WHITE CROSSES

One day when our children were small, we were traveling home from a vacation in northern California. As we made our way along the highway, our kids spied something beside the road they didn't understand. On a windswept hillside about one hundred yards off the highway were thousands of white crosses standing in perfect rank and file.

"Daddy, what is that?" one of my children asked. It occurred to me that younger generations can grow up without understanding why they have the freedom to drive along a highway . . . or to sit safely in our home . . . or to worship at a church we love.

So I took time to explain to them the significance of that hillside. In language they could understand, I told them that the brave women and men under those crosses paid the ultimate price for our liberty. "All around the world there are cemeteries like that," I said, "just as beautiful as this one."

Then I quoted from John McCrae's timeless poem: "In Flanders Fields the poppies blow/Between the crosses row on row/That mark our place . . ."—I couldn't even finish the poem, as I was moved to tears.

Perhaps you know of those who died in battle. In paying the ultimate price, they did what they considered their duty, never expecting to be applauded for it. Most people will never know their story, but God never missed one minute of it.

There are certain scenes that, whenever I come across them, always cause me to pause and let the wonder in. A row of white crosses in a military cemetery is one of those places. My children, now grown with families of their own, share that wonder with me.

79

Finding Justice in Injustice

GOD WILL BRING INTO JUDGMENT BOTH THE RIGHTEOUS AND
THE WICKED, FOR THERE WILL BE A TIME FOR EVERY ACTIVITY,
A TIME TO JUDGE EVERY DEED. —ECCLESIASTES 3:17 NIV

⁓

IT'S NOT OFTEN, FATHER, *that we make such a statement.
But today we thank You for the injustices in life that have crippled us
and broken us and crushed us. Unfair circumstances have bruised us
deeply and beaten us into submission to You. Inequities have brought
us to such a dead end that we couldn't see how to back out. The only
direction we can look is up. We often think that our unjust circumstance has ruined our lives . . . when instead, it could be the means
You have ordained to give us life. Father, if those people we know
who have trudged through the valley of the shadow of death were not
alive today, walking with You and telling us to keep going, where
would we be? How much we need their example and encouragement!
Thank You for each one.*

In light of Your sovereign grace, we thank You for blindness, for paralysis, for loss, for death, for broken dreams, for dissolved partnerships, and for disillusionment. In faith we praise You for times of insecurity, failure, divorce, and even when others have treated us unjustly. We see the storm, but You enable us to see beyond the storm, so we trust You to make all things just in Your time. You sovereignly intend for good what others intentionally meant for evil.

We pray for those facing the frustration of injustice in these and dozens of other categories. We ask that they may be able to find in Jesus Christ the strength to go on . . . especially those who have almost decided to give up. We pray that they will offer everything to You in full surrender. Everything. In the name of Jesus Christ, the Conqueror, we pray. Amen.

See also Genesis 50:20; Psalm 23:4; Psalm 119:71;
Ecclesiastes 3:11; Romans 8:28; 2 Corinthians 1:3–7.

LET'S BE ILLOGICAL

Forgive the way this sounds, but God's logic seems a little weird at times. Nobody likes to admit it aloud, but we all *think* it, right? His logic seems illogical. Stop and think about that before you toss it aside for fear of feeling like a heretic. What better answer do you have for those events that defy explanation?

We wonder why some babies are born healthy and others with special needs. Or why the godly, healthy young man gets cancer. How about the number of religious charlatans who run free? Or the brutal extermination of six million Jews in World War II. And the inequity of a precious child beaten by a drunken mom or dad.

Don't you wonder about such things? Not one "makes sense."

Ready for a shocker? We're not supposed to have airtight answers! Why? Because our understanding is earthbound . . . human to the core . . . limited . . . finite. We operate in a dimension totally unlike our Lord, who knows no limitations. We see now. He sees forever. We judge on the basis of the temporal; He, on the basis of the eternal. We try to make each piece fit into our boxes called Equity or Fairness. Not God. His logic is inscrutable, unsearchable—and yes, illogical.

And so? We *accept* rather than explain. We *trust* rather than try to make it all fit together. It helps to remember that each generation has only a few of the pieces, *none* of which may fit into one another. So stop trying to wrap everything in neat boxes.

Let's be illogical about life for a change. Otherwise, we try to play God's role. And we're all fresh out of omniscience.

80

Learning Humility

CLOTHE YOURSELVES WITH HUMILITY TOWARD ONE
ANOTHER, FOR GOD IS OPPOSED TO THE PROUD, BUT GIVES
GRACE TO THE HUMBLE. THEREFORE HUMBLE YOURSELVES
UNDER THE MIGHTY HAND OF GOD, THAT HE MAY
EXALT YOU AT THE PROPER TIME. —1 PETER 5:5–6

FATHER, WE ALL HAVE *our hopes and aspirations. We all have our dreams. And though there is nothing wrong with these, how easy it is to be driven by them. How easy to feel such expectations that if our dreams don't come true we've somehow not been loved by You. We've been trained to take care of ourselves—a fine idea that has gone to seed. It's all about* my *stuff,* my *rights,* my *promotion,* my *salary,* my *place,* my *name . . . how ugly! How un-Christian. We acknowledge before You that this life is not about us or our expectations.*

Thank You that You never miss a person. When it's time for promotion, You won't be late. When it's time for rewards, You won't forget. So, at this awesome moment, we bow before Your mighty throne. We acknowledge that You've been good to us when we've not deserved it. You've cared for us when we've been careless. You've loved us when we've been terribly unloving, and You've met our needs when we didn't even stop to think about what we ought to be giving to You and Your work. You faithfully and graciously and constantly pour out Your good things upon us. Thank You for Your deliverance. Thank You for Your disciplines.

Teach us in these tender days the value of genuine humility—of a self-forgetful life. We ask this so that we might become for You messengers whose message makes sense because our lives are like Your Son's life—the One who is gentle and humble of heart. We pray in His name, for His glory. Amen.

See also Matthew 11:29; 16:21–26; Luke 14:11; Philippians 2:3–8.

ACTING MEDIUM

The children worked long and hard on their little cardboard shack. It was to be a special spot—a clubhouse where they could meet and have fun. As they thought about their rules, they came up with three rather perceptive ones: "Nobody act big. Nobody act small. Everybody act medium."

Just "act medium." Believable, honest, thoughtful, down-to-earth. Regardless of your elevated position or high pile of honors or list of degrees or endless achievements, just stay real. Trash any idea that you deserve some kind of special recognition for a job well done. Who did you do it for anyway? If you did it for God, He has an infinite number of unseen ways to reward you. If you did it for man, no wonder you're seeking the glory! But it's so easy to seek praise for yourself, isn't it?

Remember what Solomon wrote? "Let another praise you, and not your own mouth; a stranger, and not your own lips" (Proverbs 27:2). Meaning what? Meaning no self-reference to some enviable accomplishment. Meaning refusal to scratch a back when yours itches. Meaning authentic surprise when applauded.

One final warning. Don't try to fake it. False humility stinks worse than raw conceit. The answer is not in trying to appear worthless and "wormy" but in consistently taking notice of others' achievements, recognizing others' skills and contributions . . . and saying so. That's one way to serve others in love. Like Christ.

Got the rules memorized? "Nobody act big. Nobody act small. Everybody act medium." Such good advice from a clubhouse full of kids who, by the way, are pretty good at practicing what they preach.

81

Guarding against Legalism

JESUS SAID, "GET UP, TAKE YOUR BEDROLL, START WALKING."
THE MAN WAS HEALED ON THE SPOT. HE PICKED UP HIS
BEDROLL AND WALKED OFF. THAT DAY HAPPENED TO BE
THE SABBATH. THE JEWS STOPPED THE HEALED MAN AND
SAID, "IT'S THE SABBATH. YOU CAN'T CARRY YOUR BEDROLL
AROUND. IT'S AGAINST THE RULES." —JOHN 5:8–10 MSG

———————— ༑ ————————

HEAVENLY FATHER, IT IS *our deep desire to glorify Your name.
We want to honor Your Word, even when it squares off against our
own feelings or experiences. We thank You for being kind enough
to teach us the basic things about grace. And we pray that teaching
might result in freedom from the bondage that has held captive some
of Your people far too long.*

*Now we ask for several things—that You would guard us from
extremism; that You would guard us from misunderstanding; that
You would guard Your children from foolish, licentious living; and*

that You would guard us from a misappropriation of freedom. And,

Father, we ask that You would guard those of us who are list makers

from thinking that our lists make us more holy. Deal first with our

attitude, our Father, then with our lives—whether it's for salvation,

or for deliverance from the terrible plague of legalism, or simply for

the joy of living free in Christ.

We ask it in the name that is above all names, Jesus Himself.

Amen.

See also Matthew 23:23; Galatians 5:1; 1 Peter 2:16.

COMPROMISE

In the ranks of twenty-first-century Christianity, there is a pocket of people who take pride in being ultrawhatever. Conservative to the core, and opinionated to the point of distraction, these folks are not open to discuss crucial issues or even to hear ideas from the other side. In order to guard against any subtle inroad of heresy, they refuse to think outside the boundaries of self-imposed rules.

To these legalists, compromise is a term of weakness. If you listen to people outside the camp, they might influence you. If you don't agree with the guru who calls all the shots (yes, all), then it is clear you are compromising the truth. If you fail to keep the list exactly as the group dictates—regardless of the lack of biblical support for such a list—then, clearly, you are guilty of compromise. This is the worst kind of bondage, because it is all done under the guise of Christianity.

Don't misunderstand; there are moral and ethical standards taught in Scripture that leave no room for compromise. But compromise is much broader than that. Without compromise, disagreements cannot be settled and negotiations grind to a halt. Compromise is not always bad.

Am I saying it's easy? Or free from risk? Or that it comes naturally? No. It is much easier (and safer) to stand your ground . . . to keep on believing that your way is the best way to go and that your plan is the only plan to follow. One major problem, however: you wind up narrow-minded and alone or surrounded by bobble-headed nonthinkers. That may be safe, but it won't be very satisfying. Or Christlike.

<u>82</u>

Only for the Lonely

MAKE EVERY EFFORT TO COME TO ME SOON. . . . ONLY LUKE
IS WITH ME. PICK UP MARK AND BRING HIM WITH YOU, FOR
HE IS USEFUL TO ME FOR SERVICE. . . . AT MY FIRST DEFENSE
NO ONE SUPPORTED ME, BUT ALL DESERTED ME; MAY IT NOT
BE COUNTED AGAINST THEM. BUT THE LORD STOOD WITH ME
AND STRENGTHENED ME. —2 TIMOTHY 4:9, 11, 16–17

———————— ༶ ————————

OUR FATHER, WE ACKNOWLEDGE *that we need You, and*
our need is not partial; it's total. It's not occasional; it's always—
today especially. We pray for those who wrestle with the very real
problem of loneliness. It's not dated; it surfaces regularly in every
generation. We pray especially for those who are lonely because they
are distant from You. We ask You to bring them to a knowledge of
Your Son and keep them restless and sleepless and struggling until
they have come to that place of faith in Your Son.

Thank You for meeting our every need. We pray that You will meet this one today wherever we find ourselves. And that You will show Yourself strong where we are weak, mighty where we are lacking. Meet the deep needs of our hearts, our Father, and enable us to get through the difficulty of loneliness by Your grace. In the name of Christ, our Lord, our Savior, our Master, and our God, we pray. Amen.

See also Psalm 25:16–17; 68:6; 107:4–6.

BRIDGES

Her voice was weak and fearful on the phone. Her desperate story broke my heart. Her parents didn't want her when she was born. They placed her in a foster home and walked out of her life. Years passed, and she decided she would go and find *them*. Through an incredible chain of events, she walked back into their lives one evening but soon discovered she still wasn't wanted.

Her parents allowed her to stay for a while, but one morning they announced they were going to adopt a baby boy—and "start over." Reluctantly, she squeezed out the words: "I don't want to be in your way. Maybe I'd better leave." To which her dad quickly replied, "Okay, I'll help you pack." Since that dark moment, she's slept in alleys and looked unsuccessfully for work. Wanting neither pity nor a handout, she hung up the phone because she was cold in that phone booth and needed to find shelter before the police picked her up. I will never forget her voice.

I am convinced we have in our churches those who feel unwanted, forgotten, unloved—and lonelier than words can express. Strange as it sounds, these are often the ones most difficult to love. Because of their repulsive self-image, it is only natural that they *act* repulsively. Their unpleasant lifestyle isolates them and confirms their feelings.

Instead of loving these people, we usually label them. Instead of caring, we tend to criticize. Instead of getting next to them, we react, we resent, we run. I urge you to open your heart *and your home!* Bridges aren't built with just a handshake at church or a smile as you get into your car after the worship service. Loving the unlovely is risky; it takes time and extra effort. Availability is not optional. It's essential.

<u>83</u>

Strong Marriages

HUSBANDS, LOVE YOUR WIVES, JUST AS CHRIST ALSO LOVED THE
CHURCH AND GAVE HIMSELF UP FOR HER. . . . SO HUSBANDS OUGHT
ALSO TO LOVE THEIR OWN WIVES AS THEIR OWN BODIES. HE WHO
LOVES HIS OWN WIFE LOVES HIMSELF. . . . AND THE WIFE MUST SEE
TO IT THAT SHE RESPECTS HER HUSBAND. —EPHESIANS 5:25, 28, 33

LORD, TODAY WE ARE LIVING *in a culture that has forgotten*
Your pattern for marriage. The world has lost its way because Your
Word is being ignored. We have gotten the threads of that divine
tapestry all mixed up, and the whole thing is a mess. Furthermore,
our culture is a total disaster. The fracturing of homes has become
so commonplace we no longer even raise our eyebrows when we
hear of another family that goes under. We pray, therefore, that the
truths of the words above, presented from Your exacting pattern,
the Word of God, would find root and bear fruit in some lives. We
also pray that You'd give husbands and wives the courage to say,

"I am wrong. I am sorry. Please forgive me. Let's start over." We ask that You would give partners who hear those words a renewed capacity to believe their spouses, to work alongside them, to help make Your design a reality.

Thank You, Father, for Jesus, who is here for us, who loves us, and who modeled sacrificial love on our behalf. Help us, Lord, as we live out His life in our marriages through the enabling power of Your Spirit. Through Christ our Lord, we pray. Amen.

See also Genesis 2:23–25; Mark 10:5–9; 1 Corinthians 7:1–9; Hebrews 13:4.

COMING HOME

Can it really be more than fifty-eight years? From the time Cynthia and I said "I do" to this very day, we've continued to grow as a couple. I'm so glad we've been willing to forgive each other as we stoked the fires of love together. I'm so thankful we refused to give up and walk away, to talk it through and stick it out.

Coming home reminds me of the importance of continuing to work on my marriage. I mean things like showing common courtesy, fighting petty acts of selfishness, being more understanding, listening better, forgiving quicker, talking truth, cultivating deep intimacy, resisting passivity, and a dozen other marital disciplines that keep the cobwebs swept away. They keep coming back, those ugly spiders of neglect. As I get older I want our marriage to get better, but that never "just happens." Age is no friend of affection. A healthy marriage requires hard work.

It hit me that someday—some dreadful day—either Cynthia or I will come home *alone*. I loathe the thought, but I cannot, I dare not ignore it. And when that dark night becomes a reality, I don't want any bad *I wish I had* . . . thoughts to add guilt to my grief. And so, I want to go on record by saying that I recommit myself to obeying the command, "Husbands, love your wives, just as Christ also loved the church" (Ephesians 5:25).

To all husbands everywhere, I urge you to join me in this high and holy pursuit—to make the love of our wives our aim so that coming home might always be our delight, never our dread. As that happens, we need never to fear death. On the contrary, such a pursuit will help us start to live.

84

A Prayer for Mothers

As one whom his mother comforts, so I
will comfort you. —Isaiah 66:13

———————— ⁓ ————————

WE DO WORSHIP YOU, *our Father, and in our worship we*
give You our thanks. We thank You, not only for our own mothers
and grandmothers but for all women who have filled that role. We
remember those who are now deceased, who helped shape our lives,
who taught us faithfully, and who enduringly loved us. Thank You
for the contribution of fine women all over this world who live lives
dedicated to Your service, to their families, to their extended families.
Thank You for each. You have written in Your Word that their worth
is far above jewels.

Thank You for the tenderness and compassion mothers contribute
to a world that's cold and raw and careless and harsh. Thank You for
their affirmation and words of affection in the midst of a society bent

on high achievement, self-serving goals, and short-sighted pursuits. Thank You for their hours of investment in others. Thank You for their contribution to You in the work of the church down through the centuries. Thank You for using women through the ages to improve their homes, their families, and others' lives. Thank You for their vision, for their strength of character. Most of all, for their hearts, tender to You and affectionate toward those they love.

Dear Father, so many of these things represent Your wisdom, which is, as You have written, more precious than silver—better than gold. In light of that, we rededicate ourselves to Your work, to Your service, and to those who need our love. We commit our future to You for however many months or years You may give us. May we faithfully and relentlessly serve the Master. In the name of the Savior, we pray. Amen.

See also Exodus 20:12; Proverbs 3:13–14; 6:20; 20:20; 30:17; 31:10.

———————— ‿ ————————

THE INFLUENCE OF A MOTHER

I know of no more permanent imprint on a life than the one made by a mother. She's usually the one who invests the most time and energy in the children, who understands them when they cannot fully explain their actions, and who provides the lap and the hugs when they get hurt. In case you question that, when's the last time you saw a crying child run to his *father* for consolation? When that happens, it's usually because his *mother* isn't there! The mother's influence is so great that we model it even when we don't realize it, and we return to it even to the surprise of others.

As I think of my mother's influence on me, two words come to mind: *class* and *zest*. My mother, being a classy lady, was determined to keep our family from being ignorant of the arts or lacking in social graces. I have her to thank for my love of artistic beauty, fine music, which fork to use, and keeping gravy off my tie. She also possessed such an endless zest for life! I am indebted to her for my enthusiasm and relentless drive. Her indomitable spirit got passed on, thank goodness.

My mother wasn't perfect, and neither is yours. Regardless, I hope my words make you think about the mother who has influenced you.

And if you are a mother, I urge you to call to mind the lasting legacy of your imprint. The kids may seem ungrateful, they may act irresponsible, they may even ignore your reminders and forget your advice these days. But believe this, they can never erase your influence.

Tough as it may seem today, motherhood is worth it. It is noble. It is consistent with God's kingdom. And we admire you for it!

85

Facing Our Own Death

I AM THE RESURRECTION AND THE LIFE; HE WHO BELIEVES IN
ME WILL LIVE EVEN IF HE DIES, AND EVERYONE WHO LIVES
AND BELIEVES IN ME WILL NEVER DIE. —JOHN 11:25–26

OUR FATHER, THIS IS A SACRED MOMENT *because we all
must answer the question, "Am I ready to die?" Not until we're ready
to die are we truly ready to live.*

*We acknowledge that death is the last thing we want to think
about, but thank You for bringing us face-to-face with reality. Thank
You for the gift of living on earth and the reminder that our days are
fleeting. Make us ready for the harsh moments that are before us,
calm our spirits, and remove our fears.*

*Thank You for Jesus Christ, who is the answer beyond the grave.
This day, we acknowledge Him as Lord and Savior of life and death.*

Now unto Him that is able to keep us from falling, and to present us faultless before the presence of His glory with exceeding joy, to the only wise God our Savior, be glory and majesty, dominion and power, both now and ever. For Christ is risen indeed. In His name we pray. Amen.

See also Psalm 90:12; 116:15; Romans 8:23; Hebrews 9:27; Jude 24–25.

THE FINAL TOLL

As I kissed Cynthia good night, I held her in my arms and whispered, "I cannot imagine going through such a deep valley." She agreed. It was a tender moment that stayed with me. I've never forgotten that evening, though it occurred more than twenty years ago.

Sleep came hard that night, which for me is a rarity. I'm usually out in less than ten seconds. I must have been awake another hour and a half . . . thinking, musing, praying, reviewing our many years together.

Earlier that evening, we had enjoyed a quiet meal. After supper we read together a friend's gracious, understated letter. He wrote that he and his wife had recently discovered she had inoperable cancer. In spite of their shock, they had complete confidence in God, who would soon bring her home to be with Him.

Naturally, after reading the letter, our hearts went out to our friends. His words left us pensive. In silence, we dressed for bed, each lost in nostalgia. I'm sure we were thinking the same thing: it could happen to us. If it does, I know this . . . I would not be nearly as brave as my friend, certainly not as eloquent in expressing deep feelings. Facing finality with authentic faith is a rarity. Many people mouth it . . . our friends meant it.

That night, in the arms of my wife, I couldn't help but imagine the night that ominous final bell will toll. I felt a thick knot in my throat as I tried to picture life without my loving partner . . . those long nights when the other side of my bed will be cold and empty . . . when lonely memories will replace close companionship. And, with a prayer of gratitude for our life together, I fell asleep.

86

Finding Rest in God

On God my salvation and my glory rest; the rock
of my strength, my refuge is in God. Trust in Him
at all times, O people; pour out your heart before
Him; God is a refuge for us. —Psalm 62:7–8

Our dear Father, we are grateful *for the rest that is
found in Christ. Our souls were like waves crashing against a shoreline, and our lives were in tumult and disarray, confusion and chaos.
And then You rescued us. You brought us forgiveness and relief, and
You introduced us to a wonderful four-letter word that has become for
us a lifeline for survival:* rest. *Thank You for the peace that accompanies this rest. Thank You for the freedom from worry. Thank You for
carrying the weights that we used to carry on our own shoulders, for
giving us literally thousands of promises that become ours to claim, to
grow in, and to be comforted by.*

Father, You have the ability, being who You are, to know each need in each heart, each concern in each mind. So we pause and release

to You those things that have plagued us long enough. We give them

over to You now. In doing so, we invite the Spirit of God to plow the

soil of our souls so the seed of God's Word can be sown, take root, and

be watered in time so as to produce spiritual abundance.

We commit these valued moments to You, resting in You. And

may this allow us to be lost in wonder and love and praise. In Jesus'

name, we pray. Amen.

See also Genesis 2:2–3; Joshua 21:44; Psalm 22:2–3; Ecclesiastes 9:11; Hebrews 4:9.

TIME TO REST

There is more to life than increasing its speed.

I'll never forget the day Cynthia and I got snowed in. The rain that fell by buckets along the coast turned into a mild snow-and-ice storm up in the mountains. Temperatures dropped to the midtwenties. The wind outside the windows howled with gusts up to forty miles an hour where we were for a couple of days. And suddenly in the midst of it all, our electricity went on the blink.

No lights. No heat. No phone. Only a fireplace to keep warm by and an old Coleman lantern and a flashlight to see with. Our rugged existence lasted about twenty-four hours. Both our projects were put on hold. As the stacks of work sat idly by, we sat in front of the fire . . . warming our feet as we cooled our jets. For a while, my internal transmission was still set on "drive" and my mind was fretting over the lost opportunity to get something done. Finally, I realized (after some honest talk time) we weren't mistakenly stranded at Paradise Lost but magnificently marooned on Paradise Found. Quiet. Still. Able to talk in depth with no concern for time, any interruption, or deadline. Life slowed to a standstill . . . it was obviously time to rest, regardless of the agenda we had arranged.

As the snow fell and stuck to the windowpanes, I stared into the flickering flames. A line from Solomon's journal flashed across my mind: "The race is not to the swift" (Ecclesiastes 9:11). Clearly, it was the Father's sovereign will that this husband and wife deliberately stop striving, stop rushing, stop fretting, stop doing—and simply rest.

We did. I'm glad.

87

Honoring God's Sovereignty

HE DOES ACCORDING TO HIS WILL IN THE HOST OF
HEAVEN AND AMONG THE INHABITANTS OF EARTH; AND
NO ONE CAN WARD OFF HIS HAND OR SAY TO HIM,
"WHAT HAVE YOU DONE?" —DANIEL 4:35

SOVEREIGN GOD, ALL OF US *would be quick to say that we do need to be relieved of our anxieties—they are too many and too frequent. And because we want to call our own shots, we need to be leveled and removed from the realm of pride.*

Help us stop feeling as though we need an explanation of why, as life unfolds around us. Show us again, Lord, that You are God and there is no other—that You are in the heavens; You do whatever You please. You are at work in our lives, in the lives of our neighbors, in the lives of those who live across the street, across the country, and across the seas. You are at work. No one else is in charge, and You do all things well. You change the times and the seasons. You also change us.

Make Your Word as relevant as tomorrow morning's news on the Internet, as significant as what we would read in the daily paper. And bring us back to the recognition of Your sovereignty, Father: that we answer to You because You are our all in all.

Today we worship Your Son as Lord, and we worship Your name as the one and only true God through whom, thankfully, we have a salvation that is eternal and secure. We rest in these truths as Your children.

We also remember those who have never met Your Son as Savior. Give them unrest, uneasiness, even sleepless nights until they find their peace and rest in knowing You . . . and not in understanding their circumstances. May they believe in You through faith in Christ, in whose name we pray. Amen.

See also Genesis 50:20; Job 40:1–5; Psalm 115:3; Romans 8:28; 9:20–21.

GOD'S SOVEREIGN CONTROL

Accept it or not, God is calling the shots. He's running the show. Either He's in *full* control or He's off His throne. It's as foolish to say He is "almost sovereign" as it would be to say I'm "somewhat married" or a woman is "sort of pregnant."

We shall never be able to grasp all the ramifications of this great truth. Trying to unravel all the knots can turn you into a fanatical freak . . . it will push you beyond your mental capacity . . . it will result in endless hours of theological hairsplitting. The finite can *never* plumb the depths of the infinite . . . so don't waste your time trying. There's no way you'll ever fully reconcile God's election and man's responsibility . . . the justice of God and the injustices of man . . . our Lord's supreme control and this earth's inequities and tragedies. No way.

It was a glorious day when I was freed from the fear of saying, "I don't understand the reasons why, but I accept God's hand in what has happened." It was a *greater* day when I realized that nobody expected me to have all the answers—least of all, God! If I could figure it all out, I'd qualify as His advisor, and Scripture makes it clear that He doesn't need my puny counsel. He wants my unreserved love, my unqualified devotion, my undaunted trust . . . not *my analysis of Him and His ways.*

One of the marks of spiritual maturity is the quiet confidence that God is in complete control . . . without the need to understand or explain why He does what He does.

88

Pure Motives in Service

GOD HAS PLACED THE MEMBERS, EACH ONE OF THEM, IN THE BODY, JUST AS HE DESIRED. IF THEY WERE ALL ONE MEMBER, WHERE WOULD THE BODY BE? BUT NOW THERE ARE MANY MEMBERS, BUT ONE BODY. —1 CORINTHIANS 12:18–20

FATHER, YOU MADE ALL OF US *with different personalities, with different gifts and responsibilities, yet You choose to mingle us together in the same body of believers, over which Christ is Head. You provide us endless opportunities to give of ourselves, to teach others, to guide the confused, to help those in need, and to carry the burdens of others. As we serve Your people and touch the lives of those outside the church, we face great temptations to be in charge, to force others to get in line, to make things more uniform and rigid, to get narrow and demanding, to set our expectations too high, to handle the work of ministry and life in general as if they were secular enter- prises. God, we need You to keep things fresh and unpredictable and especially to keep us authentic, servant-hearted people who are easy to live with. Remind us that You are the Potter and we are the clay.*

So give us new hope . . . hope beyond religion, hope that motivates us to press on, to serve You with pure motives, strong minds, and humble hearts. Thank You for Your grace, our only hope . . . in Jesus' name. Amen.

See also Acts 2:44–47; 9:31; 1 Corinthians 11:16; 12:1–31; Philippians 2:3–4.

------------------------------ ⌣ ------------------------------

BECOMING PEACEMAKERS

D o you realize how closely unity and humility are tied together? One breeds the other. Neither can exist without the other. They're like Siamese twins, perpetually connected.

Personally, I have seen numerous occasions when pride won out (even though it was never called that) and harmony faded away . . . and I mean *fast*. Contrary to the stuff you might read today, the words *fight* and *quarrel* are not apt descriptions of the way to get ahead. More importantly, they don't glorify God. Friends are made (and kept) by *not* fighting and by *refusing* to quarrel.

I'm convinced we need to commit ourselves to freeing others so they can grow and discover on their own. For a change, as much as is possible, let's walk away from an argument rather than inviting one. Let's become the peacemakers Jesus urged us to be (Matthew 5:9).

Peacemakers release tension; they don't intensify it. Peacemakers seek solutions and find no delight in arguments. Peacemakers calm the waters; they don't trouble them. Peacemakers work hard to keep an offense from occurring . . . and when it does occur, they strive for resolution. Peacemakers lower their voices rather than raise them. Peacemakers generate more light than heat. Blessed are such great-hearted souls!

Make no mistake, however; *peacemaker* is not a synonym for *appeaser*. This is not peace at any price. There are boundaries we dare not trespass. Smiling or closing our eyes at wrongdoing or erroneous teaching doesn't simplify life. It complicates it.

When Christ blessed the peacemakers, He was extolling the value of doing all we can to maintain harmony and support unity. His interest was in making peace where peace is an appropriate objective.

89

Stop Fussing . . . and Focus Instead

MARY . . . SAT BEFORE THE MASTER, HANGING ON EVERY WORD
HE SAID. BUT MARTHA WAS PULLED AWAY BY ALL SHE HAD TO
DO IN THE KITCHEN. LATER, SHE STEPPED IN, INTERRUPTING
THEM. "MASTER, DON'T YOU CARE THAT MY SISTER HAS
ABANDONED THE KITCHEN TO ME? TELL HER TO LEND ME A
HAND." THE MASTER SAID, "MARTHA, DEAR MARTHA, YOU'RE
FUSSING FAR TOO MUCH. . . . ONE THING ONLY IS ESSENTIAL,
AND MARY HAS CHOSEN IT." —LUKE 10:39–42 MSG

FATHER, WE ACKNOWLEDGE *that worry is not simply a bad habit but rather, it is a sin . . . a repeated sin. Worry compromises our fellowship with You and with others. We thank You that the death of Your Son, Jesus, provided the payment in full for our sins, including the sin of worry. We trust Him to take care of our worries. As the psalmist said, we can cast our burden upon the Lord and He will sustain us. He will never allow the righteous to be shaken.*

We pray that You will quiet our hearts. As You do, please lead us to a quiet and sure confidence in Yourself. Take the things that we needlessly fuss over—those worries that have burdened us long enough—and erase them from our minds. Please teach us to focus on You instead—to sit at Your feet in quietness. And as we cast the heavy weight of anxiety on You, we will trust You to give us instead a peace that surpasses understanding and a confidence that You are at work— even though we remain in the same circumstances. Thank You ahead of time for how You will deal with the burdens that weigh heavy on our hearts. Thank You for how You will relieve the anxieties that cause us to miss the important things in life. We thank You in the name of Christ our Lord and Savior. Amen.

See also Psalm 55:22; Proverbs 12:25; Isaiah 26:3; Matthew 6:31–34; Philippians 4:6–7; 1 Peter 5:7.

HOW TO WASTE YOUR TIME

Most self-help books follow the same theme: how to get the most out of your time . . . how to increase your efficiency . . . how to make every moment count. However, I'd like to take the opposite tack for a moment and tell you how to waste your time. One proven idea is all you need: *worry a lot.*

Start worrying early in the morning and intensify your anxiety energy as the day passes. A good way to get ideas on what to worry about? The news. Search the newspaper or Internet for discouraging and negative information. Don't miss the evening news on television. For sure, constantly check your smartphone for late-breaking calamities. That way, you can spend the rest of the day churning over them.

Something I have found helpful in my own worry world is to do a lot of reflecting on my failures. If you're a parent, an excellent swamp to plunge into is stuff you did wrong with your children. Think long and hard about what you should have done but didn't. That will give guilt a green light. To add a touch of variety, you could also call to mind some things you should not have done but did. Regret and shame fuel worry. A few other categories to camp on? Your weight. The things you dislike about your marriage or job. The weather. Your finances. Hanging around negative people is another secret you won't want to forget.

When you put these suggestions in motion, you can forget about the hassles connected with being happy, efficient, and productive. Just consider the benefits of all that time wasted.

Come to think of it, I can't think of one.

90

Nativity

WHEN THE FULLNESS OF THE TIME CAME, GOD SENT FORTH HIS
SON, BORN OF A WOMAN, BORN UNDER THE LAW, SO THAT HE
MIGHT REDEEM THOSE WHO WERE UNDER THE LAW, THAT WE
MIGHT RECEIVE THE ADOPTION AS SONS. —GALATIANS 4:4–5

———————— ·ᴗ· ————————

FATHER, THANK YOU *for the greatest of all stories. We are
thrilled to read it again and again. It never gets old, because its message touches every day of our lives. Your plan of redemption is one
we claim, though we cannot fully explain. How grateful we are that
we can't! It requires faith. So by faith we believe it . . . just as Mary
believed the angel Gabriel, who appeared to her in Nazareth. Just
as You came alive in her womb through the Person of Your Son, we
pray that Your Spirit will come alive in the hearts of all who hear
and receive the message of the Savior. Like Mary, may they accept
it by faith, turning to the Lord Jesus Christ as Master of their lives.*

We also ask, our Father, that You will give us who believe the ability to rivet our mind on things above and not on things of this earth. We want Christmas to have its own beauty, its unique and profound significance, as we focus on the scene that we have looked upon so many times before. Help us to celebrate the truth, not figurines in a nativity scene, but the true Son of God who came that we might live and have eternal life with Him. It's in His matchless name that we thank You, Lord. Amen.

See also Luke 1:38; Romans 10:1; 11:33–36; Colossians 3:1–2.

IT'S ALWAYS TIME FOR GIFTS

Where is it written in the Bible that holidays are the only time to give gifts? So what if it's not the Christmas season? Who cares if Father's Day or Mother's Day or a friend's birthday won't appear on our calendars for months? It's never too early to give some gifts away.

Let me give you some ideas. Here are thirty-two suggestions; take your choice: Mend a quarrel. Seek out a forgotten friend. Dismiss suspicion. Write a long overdue love note. Hug someone tightly and whisper, "I love you." Forgive an enemy. Be gentle and patient with an angry person. Express appreciation. Gladden the heart of a child. Find the time to keep a promise. Make or bake something for someone else—anonymously. Release a grudge. Listen. Speak kindly to a stranger. Enter into another's sorrow. Smile. Laugh a little. Laugh a little more. Take a walk with a friend. Kneel down and stroke a dog. Read a poem to your mate or friend. Lessen your demands on others. Play some beautiful music during supper. Apologize if you were wrong. Talk together with the television and cell phone off. Treat someone to an ice cream cone (frozen yogurt would be fine). Do the dishes for the family. Pray for someone who helped you when you hurt. Fix breakfast on Saturday morning. Give a soft answer even though you feel strongly. Encourage an older person. Point out one thing you appreciate most about someone you work with or live near. Offer to babysit for a weary mother. Give your teacher a break—be especially cooperative.

Let's make this season one long, extended gift of ourselves to others. Unselfishly. Without announcement. Or obligation. Or reservation. Or hypocrisy. That *is* Christianity, isn't it?

INDEX

WORTHY
PUBLISHING

IF YOU ENJOYED THIS BOOK, WILL YOU CONSIDER SHARING THE MESSAGE WITH OTHERS?

- Mention the book in a Facebook post, Twitter update, Pinterest pin, or blog post.

- Recommend this book to those in your small group, book club, workplace, and classes.

- Head over to facebook.com/worthypublishing, "LIKE" the page, and post a comment as to what you enjoyed the most.

- Tweet "I recommend reading #HearMeWhenICall by @chuckswindoll // @worthypub"

- Pick up a copy for someone you know who would be challenged and encouraged by this message.

- Write a review on amazon.com, bn.com, goodreads.com, or cbd.com.

You can subscribe to Worthy Publishing's newsletter at worthypublishing.com.

WORTHY PUBLISHING
FACEBOOK PAGE

WORTHY PUBLISHING
WEBSITE